&

A Christmas Carol 2

The Return of Scrooge

&

A Christmas Carol 2:

The Return of Scrooge

Third Road Press

Cover design by Bryan Larkin

Copyright © 2012 Robert J. Elisberg

ISBN-13: 978-0615727578

ISBN-10: 0615727573

To my mother,

who actually read <u>Dombey and Sons</u>
and even remembered details of it many decades later.

And my father,

who remembered pretty much everything else.

TABLE OF CONTENTS

INTRODUCTION

In 1837, Charles Dickens published the first of his novels, <u>The Posthumous Papers of the Pickwick Club</u>, and world literature took a new direction. The book became a phenomenon, and Dickens became a celebrity of renown. Remarkably, over the next four years, he not only wrote four additional novels, making it five books in five years, but all of them were prodigious successes, as well, providing you don't count <u>Barnaby Rudge</u>.

Dickens's novels were initially serialized in magazines and newspapers, and then later published in book form. The reason is because Dickens rarely had a fully-developed idea when he set out to write a book, and releasing a story one chapter at a time gave him the liberty to improvise at length before he could figure out what he was actually writing about. When later published as novels, this was rarely a problem since most of the public had read the story already, so they could skim the opening 100 pages or so without missing anything. As later generations came to the novels without the benefit of having read them beforehand in serial format, this was no longer an issue because by that point Dickens was long-since considered an Important Artist, so the obscurity of those first 100 indecisive pages was seen as evidence of his layered substance and genius.

Perhaps the most pronounced features of Dickens' novels was their length. This was the result of two causes. The first is that, being serials initially, Dickens wasn't hindered by the burden of needing to turn in a completed story with an actual ending, so he could go on and on at length until whenever he decided to stop. The second reason is that Dickens was paid by the word.

By the time 1843 came, Dickens had been approached to write a Christmas story. As this would be intended for a specific season, clearly the author wouldn't have the luxury of telling a tale with an open ending that could run ramblingly until Easter. He needed a short (by Dickens's standards) story that could be not just published, but most importantly read for the holiday.

The result was <u>A Christmas Carol</u>. It quickly became one of the most beloved holiday stories ever written, in part for the beauty of its telling and its heart-enriching message, and in part because of its brevity, which enthralled his grateful reading public.

As sales of the short book rose to majestic heights, a publisher, McCreevey Hamilton & Sons, Ltd., came to Dickens with a novel idea. Or so Dickens thought, but it wasn't for a new novel at all, but yet another Christmas novella. The publisher wanted to build on the success of the original <u>A Christmas Carol</u> and have Dickens write a sequel.

Although he had never written a sequel before, Dickens leapt at the opportunity. As he explained in his return letter, this was for the creative challenge, as well as the especially large advance payment. He immediately set to work, and the publisher assigned one of the company's most experienced and beloved partners, Sir Joseph Bunderston, to oversee the effort.

Though the undertaking began with boundless enthusiasm and hearty good fellowship, over time the working relationship between the two men, as well as the publishing house soured. Because of creative and personal recriminations by each side, along with disagreements on the contract, the resulting book was never released. Eventually, Dickens himself shelved the story and instead went back to quickly write a completely different Christmas story, <u>The Chimes</u>, for his original publisher. Because it had been thrown together so fast, it was by necessity even shorter than <u>A Christmas Carol</u>, something which became the standard for all his subsequent Christmas stories. Thanks its popularity, Dickens went on to write a new Christmas tale every year for many years to come, each one generally shorter than the previous.

Amid all of his great success, Dickens's sequel to <u>A Christmas Carol</u> sat unseen for almost 170 years, and was believed to be long lost. The manuscript was only recently discovered by scholars in the basement of a boarding house in the city of York. How it got there, no one is quite sure, although the rudimentary stick-figure drawings on the back of each page give supporting evidence that it may have been used as a children's coloring book. Either that, or Dickens' own random doodlings were significantly less mature than his writing.

But how mature that writing is. Charles Dickens was the most respected and popular author of his era. Indeed, readers seemed to hang on his every word, waiting anxiously for the next monthly installment to be released. Observers at the time, even among Dickens's greatest admirers, marveled in disbelief that there were members of the public so fanatical that they would actually line up for days ahead of the release of a new Dickens publication, standing outside of stores in long lines, just for the sake of being first. And his popularity remarkably has continued through generations, beyond the barriers of the ages.

With the passage of time, however, literature often gets obscured by the cloudy lens of history, and some references in his work have become foreign to later readers (from which comes the phrase, "What the Dickens is he talking about??"). As a result, footnotes throughout this text guide the reader through unfamiliar characters, names and events of the period. They are comprised of Dickens's personal notes written on his manuscript, letters from his publisher Sir Joseph Bunderston, Dickens's own correspondence, and scholarly commentary by the editor of this newly-published volume.

Robert J. Elisberg
B.S.S., Northwestern University
MFA, UCLA
2012

(Publisher's note: Our researchers have been unable to find evidence of any claims that the author makes for the existence of the original manuscript he says Charles Dickens wrote. However, though he has yet to provide documentation that it actually existed, and while profound skepticism exists among scholars, Mr. Elisberg insists it's all true, and we're inclined to go along with him. The company has a great deal invested in this project. We have been advised by our legal department that if it turns out we're wrong, since Mr. Dickens passed away in 1870, we're on pretty solid ground against a lawsuit.)

Stave One

THE GHOST

Scrooge was alive. Alive in the hearts of those who cherished the old gentleman following his joyful re-birth that wonderful Christmas past. Alive in the soul of mankind that weaves amongst us all. Alive in the minds of every person who knew him little yet was touched by his late benevolence.

In all other respects though he was dead. Mind you, when visitors stopped by his home that Christmas Eve and saw him unmoving in his favorite high-backed chair, they thought nothing of it. "Old Scrooge, napping again," they whispered and departed. After several days, though, it became clear that Dear Ebenezer had most truly himself departed and earned the Greatest Rest of all.

So, make no mistake, Scrooge was indeed dead. As I sit here before you, sincere in my gaze between friends, that is a certainty as sure as the sun emblazoning acrosst the heavens each day. He was dead. Inspected, carried off, notarized, buried, dead. Dead, dead, dead.

Oh, my, the funeral was a hard day for Bob Cratchit. In the time since that fateful eve when Scrooge had learned the Meaning of Christmas, his former clerk had become Scrooge's best friend, most-trusted associate, legal executor, political advisor, fishing companion, and singing collaborator on those nights when Scrooge wished to partake in a good old duet. For seven years, their friendship blossomed so richly until Scrooge saw Bob as the son he never had, and Bob in his turn saw Scrooge as the father he never had, except for his own father.

When Scrooge finally passed to the Eternal World five years ago this very night to join again his former partner Jacob Marley, he left his estate to his nephew Fred. However, his thriving counting-house business did Scrooge entrust to Cratchit, who considered Fred a particularly flighty sort but thought the bequest right and proper regardless. Family is family, after all, the lesson at the heart of Everything.

Nephew Fred felt the very same about family and believed therefore that the firm too should have gone to him. But as months passed, he realized that Time heals all wounds and that the fortune left by his uncle allowed him to travel, play and do as he pleased, something not possible had he been deskbound at an office. And as what most pleased him was being elected to Parliament, the last thing he needed was yet another responsibility.

And so Bob Cratchit ran Scrooge and Marley's. If ever it could be said that the public loved a business, that business was Scrooge and Marley's. Bob Cratchit learned from his benefactor that to lend someone money was to give them hope. No law dictated how low an interest rate could be enacted, no chiseled commandment decreed how long a loan must take to be paid back..

So too did Bob Cratchit's good heart extend upon all mankind Charity at its most philanthropic. Business is business, Bob knew, but he was often heard saying that the heart does itself good by doing good for its own good. If open-hearted charity meant that business profits were less, then so be it, he avowed, for there is no limit on the profits of the soul.

A better man than Bob Cratchit was hard to find. "The day to you, Bob," people would cry out as he passed along the cobbled streets, for his presence brought smiles to all who knew him, and even to those who knew him not. The more Cratchit gave, the richer he was. And if that be one of Life's mysteries, it is perhaps its most beauteous. So, to say it again, a better man than Bob Cratchit was hard to find.

*

Once upon a time – a bitterly cold Christmas Eve it was, the very same as another time upon once twelve years before – Bob Cratchit sat at his cluttered desk in his cluttered room of his cluttered office unable to work, filled with excitement for the season that was but nine hourly strokes away. As the chimes of the office tolled three, a light snow fell outside the window. But for Cratchit, when it was Christmastime, he could only see the holiday in front of his nose. "Bless my soul," thought Cratchit, "if I'm not about to burst at such a time as this, then call me a liar." And no one ever called Cratchit a liar, except for that one time when he broke his good wife's favorite china vase and blamed it on a neighbour's dog who, as dog's go, was unable to defend itself. But for the most part, Bob Cratchit was as good as his word in this good old world.

In the back nook of the office, the three clerks were unable to work either. For them, however, it was for reasons very different. Try as they might to concentrate, the heat from the main room was sweltering. Filled all day with red coals, the iron stove gave forth rippling waves enough to melt a village of igloos.

The young clerks had removed their outer coats which helped somewise, but even rolling up their sleeves had its limitations in providing relief. The youngest of them, a lanky apprentice with tousled hair and a kindly but driven way about him, was diligent in his work, yet sweat kept dripping from his brow and smearing his figures upon the holiday reports. "Oh, bosh," he said quietly. "I have to check over all the original accounts again now." The others would have commiserated, but they were wearily fanning themselves with whatever ledgers were handy.

Fidgeting away at his desk, for at Christmas season he was a schoolboy full of giddy anticipation, Bob Cratchit's restless mind wandered from the balance sheet before him to visions of sugarplums and then a quenching holiday mug of Smoking Bishop. Finally, he forced himself to focus on the matter at hand, how much at year's end should he gift the needy. For even though the firm's proceeds were down from a twelvemonth before, Cratchit believed that that was what made charity all the more meaningful.

The sound of a thud came from the back room and broke Cratchit's concentration, though that was not a terribly difficult thing to do today. "What ho?" he called out, "What was that"?

"If I may be ever so bold, sir, I do believe possibly

4

that perhaps one of the young clerks has fainted," his head clerk out front replied meekly.

Cratchit quickly moved across the room.

"Bless my soul, John Greevey," Cratchit sang out to the young man now weakly straggling to his feet. "You are lightheaded from the season, no doubt! I know the feeling well, my boy. It may be dog's cold outside, but I feel only warmth in my heart."

Mr. Greevey's associate, the hard-working, young, tousle-haired apprentice, began to defend his compatriot, but the others quickly stopped him. They knew well that when Mr. Cratchit was in such a mood, it was best to leave providence as it was. With no difficulty, Cratchit could go into a 40-minute address on the need to provide.

"Beautifully said, Mr. Cratchit, so very beautifully spoken. I wish I could orate as well, I do so wish," called the head clerk from out in the front office. An older man than the other three, he was gaunt with an almost-hunched way of carrying himself, his hair slicked back in an oily manner, which indeed was his whole manner, period. "But such fine words will never be mine, for I am oh-so 'umble, and you are ever-so noble."

The young men rolled their eyes at the painful obsequiousness of the little man and did all they could to keep from choking on their loathing. "Oh, well, every office does need someone like that, I suppose," sighed the middle clerk, Joe Noggle his name was. "But I would accept God's will if that man died a horrible death."

"'Umble, I am. 'Umble, 'Umble," the head clerk continued. "Oh, ever 'umble."

Cratchit took full measure of the man. "So you say every day, and each day I tell you nay. And this day before the birth of He who made us all noble, I say to you with full heart – Uriah Heep[1], you are as noble inside as All Men who walk the earth!"

---

[1] Uriah Heep

Editor's note.   Although known for his noble social conscience, Dickens also had a famously thin skin that rarely forgot a personal slight.   When he was an apprentice reporter in the law courts, Dickens was set to get a highly-anticipated promotion at a time he most needed the income.   However, another clerk advanced ahead of him by virtue of what Dickens wrote to a friend was, "flattery to his superiors so squeezingly unctuous it once made two clerks ill, deception so venal that calling it a high crime is being polite, and a false modesty so overwrought that it embarrassed the concept of false modesty.   The job should have been mine."   Even though he wrote this 20 years after the fact, and it was his inability to get that very promotion that propelled Dickens to become a famous novelist, whenever he could mock the fellow Dickens did.   He used him as the basis of the character of Uriah Heep in this story, but always felt he didn't go far enough, and brought Heep back in David Copperfield.   Later, Dickens had a series of posters plastered throughout London that mocked the man. And he left behind notes for a proposed book, The Brutal but Well-Deserved Death of Uriah Heep, though scholars are uncertain if this was for a serious work or just playful wish-fulfillment by the author.

A series of loud, gargled coughs and hacks came from the back room, which Cratchit believed may have been the popping crackle of the fire. Yes, he thought to himself, today of all days is good and grand and fine because it lets us look to the future, for the future of today is tomorrow, and tomorrow is Christmas.

With the tinkle of a bell, the front door to the office opened, letting in a blast of cold air that blessedly permeated the workplace. Entering was Scrooge's nephew, Fred, his hair neatly cut in the latest fashion and showing touches of gray under a tall hat, though no hat can hide the passing of time.

"Fred! Fred!," cried out Cratchit, overjoyed to see Scrooge's relative, for it was like seeing his own. "What brings you here? The season, I'm sure! The season."

"I've come, Bob," explained Fred, looking upon the worn furniture and peeling paint on the walls, "because I've heard distressing reports of the state of affairs here."

"Bless my soul, all is as well as a batter pudding."

Fred (who was feeling a bit warm now and unbuttoned his coat) scratched around the ears, not convinced, and uncertain too what was so well about batter pudding.

"If you say so, Bob, I am happy to hear it. But if you ever do decide to sell the old place…do keep my name in mind. The parts may be of value more than the whole. Better that than have my dear uncle's cherished business go under for naught."

"Oh, bless my soul," Cratchit laughed, a tear of mirth streaking down his cheek. "Sell! Ha ha ha. What good humour you give me at this time of year." Cratchit hugged the startled Fred. "Come, you must join me for Christmas dinner tomorrow! My family is vacationing up north, and I have been left a bachelor."

The nephew quickly pulled back, a look of concern on his ruddy face. "No," he replied sharply. "No. Thank you."

"But why?"

"Why?" Fred struggled to come up with a reason, other than the last place on earth he wished to be on Christmas Day was alone with the person driving a family legacy into the ground, which could also be a mark most foul on his next election campaign. "My wife and I, we are going to a retreat. A monastery. Actually, more like a cloister, something which...." Completely flustered, he knew there was only one way out of this conversation, and that was through the front door. With only a hasty nod, he made his exit quickly.

As Scrooge's nephew left, a jolly gentleman of large girth and genial bearing squeezed in. A red vest was barely buttoned upon his belly, and his brown waistcoat clung tight to his body. Removing his porkpie hat and holding it politely in his hands, he led three other oddly-shaped men in, all stamping off the cold. Their arrival kept the door wide open, and moans of thanks drifted up from the back room.

"Have I the pleasure of addressing Mr. Scrooge or Mr. Marley?" the jolly gentleman inquired of Cratchit.

"Mr. Scrooge has been dead these five years, and Mr. Marley, he passed on in..." Bob stopped, lost in thought. He turned to his secretary, dressed outlandishly in all-white flowing lace and a veil. "Miss Havisham², when in heavens *did*

---

² Miss Havisham.

Editor's note: Dickens's papers show that when he created the character of Miss Havisham, he thought the Christmas story could use some comic relief from a daft "slapdash"

8

Mr. Marley pass on?"

"Oh, Mr. Marley," the old, gray woman rhapsodized to no one in particular, as she waltzed through the room, looking around with great expectation, "my dear Mr. Marley, hello, there, you look so handsome tonight." She called across to the startled visitors, "Mr. Marley and I are to be married, you know."

"She's a fairly harmless soul, we believe," Cratchit noted to the men. "When she was burned out of her home, I took her in. It's the kind of effort we make for others."

(cont'd) character, the kind he had always loved as a boy on stage and thought wildly funny in a "panto." When the publisher first read her introduction, he was concerned that Miss Havisham was far too strange and foolishly unbelievable, though Dickens wrote that he had loosely based on a neighbor's aunt who was always wandering aimlessly into his home, often interrupting him when he was working. Dickens thought it might help the publisher's concerns if he created a backstory for her, to make her more real, and came up with Miss Havisham having had a disastrous love affair which is what drove her crazy and warped her personality into bitter vengeance. Needless-to-say, this removed some of the humorous aspects of her character, so Dickens largely dropped her from the story. He remembered her later, though, and expanded this cruelly vindictive Miss Havishman for <u>Great Expectations</u>, although he agreed to edit out the comic parts.

"The very reason we came," the jolly gentleman explained as his companions nodded vigorously. "This time of year is so difficult for many. Let me introduce myself. I am Samuel Pickwick[3], and these are my associates of the Pickwick Club, Mr. Winkle, Tupman and Snodgrass. Though I'm never quite sure which is which," he added with a wink and a chortle.

It was Bob Cratchit's great pleasure to meet them, and

---

[3] Mr. Pickwick, Tupman, Winkle and Snodgrass.

From Dickens's notes: Samuel Pickwick had been the main character of Dickens's first major success as a novelist, The Posthumous Papers of the Pickwick Club. He realized it might be surprising to include such a hugely popular character in this new, short tale, recognizing that it could make the public think it was to be a sequel. Notes in the margin express his ruminations, "Character of Mr. Pickwick was dearly beloved for his larger-than-life humor as the epitome of a good-natured and well-meaning British gentleman. However, the word 'posthumous' in title confused some of the public into believing that Mr. Pickwick had died. Want to correct any misunderstanding, so would seem best to include him in this story and show that the good fellow is very much alive." A later note in the margin adds, "Having made decision to include Mr. Pickwick, readers will be exceedingly disappointed if other members of the Pickwick Club are not also included. No idea how those members can fit into this story. However, since they don't do much in that novel, there is no great need for that to change here."

heartily shook their hands until their arms were near pulled off. "Bless my soul, I do so admire a charitable society," he enthused.

"How much of a donation may we put you down for then?

"Nothing."

"You wish to be left alone?" Snodgrass asked.

"I wish to be left anonymous," Bob shouted and went to his room, where he kept a safe and took out many large bank drafts which he stuffed in Mr. Pickwick's hand.

The kindly Pickwick was made wary by such a grandiose act of liberality, for times were very hard, and having heard of the company's struggles, he was uncertain whether Mr. Cratchit's bank would even cover the gentleman's notes.

"This appears far too generous," he politely flustered. "Indeed, your fellow money lender Mr. Dawkins said his own firm would be unable to spare even a farthing for us. So, I beg don't extend yourself beyond reason."

As several drafts were returned to him, Bob thought a moment, and then he carefully clarified the situation his petitioners faced. "Are there not other charities that compete with you for contributions?"

"Ay, there are," Tupman sighed, forced to agree. "But I wish there were not."

"Well, this money is going to be given away. To somebody. So I suggest you accept it yourselves and decrease the surplus appropriation."

With that, Cratchit shoved an extra bank note into each Pickwickian pocket and bid the men a solid "Good day!!"

Cratchit returned to his desk, when his ethereal secretary danced in. Standing behind her in the doorway was the tousled-haired and diligent apprentice clerk, appearing a bit anxious, but determined in his resolve. "Don't you forget his appointment, sir, wanting and wishing and waiting and meaning to talk to you, oh, you, just you," Miss Havisham sang out to Cratchit. "Young Mr. Twist is arrived."

"Oliver! Yes, of course, you wanted to discuss your salary. Come in, lad." Bob lavishly motioned the young man to sit, but the apprentice stayed on his feet.

"Please, sir, I want some more."

At that moment, a loud, distracting clatter came from the outer room, as another clerk collapsed to the floor. Cratchit turned an ear back in his clerk's direction, "What?!"

"I've been at Scrooge and Marley's for over two years now," the young man said with resolve. "I arrive at dawn and am here 14 hours later. I've saved many an account, Mr. Cratchit, sir. And, sir, I'm 23 years old now, and am paid almost nothing, apprentice wages. Please, sir."

Cratchit stood and loomed over the young man. "Done, as the cook said to the roast after taking it from the oven. You shall have it." He put out his hand to seal the agreement. "I'll triple your salary next week. A new start for a New Year. How's that?"

Oliver was overly-prepared to continue with his detailed presentation, as was his way, but though young, he was wise enough to know when he'd pled enough. He also had great ideas, wonderful plans, he said. The office could be so much more efficient – needed to be, in fact. He had thoughts too for investing. "And Mr. Cratchit, sir, there are matters of us being over-staffed that need to be addressed." He said no more, but had one particular, overstaffed, oily, head clerk in mind.

"All in good time, my boy, it's Christmas Eve," Bob beamed. "File this receipt, and we'll lock up early so all can go home to their loved ones as has them."

Oliver saw how much had been given to the Pickwick Club, and let out a painful groan. This was the very sort of thing they needed to discuss.

"Last one out, don't forget to douse the lamps," Cratchit called, bundling himself up already, the clock nearing but 3:45. "You'll be wanting all week off until January First, no doubt."

"What? No," Oliver immediately stopped and headed back. "Just Christmas. We'll be back on the 26th."

His fellow workers tried to hush him, but soon realized he was right. The office could ill-afford shuttering for half a fortnight, and they appealed to Cratchit.

"As you wish," the proprietor replied. "It'll be good to see your cheery faces again so soon."

The cold wind moaned outside, but inside the employees knew they had a job to come back to, and considering the season they'd been through, that was a good thing indeed.

A giddy Bob Cratchit took off down the street into the oncoming dusk and walked with such a clatter, the snow crunching under his feet, until he was out of sight. "Happy Christmas to all," his voice heard shouting back to his staff, "and to all a good night."

As he headed down the high street, Cratchit rejoiced in the pleasures of the season, but so too did the season's hardships appear to him, and in a manner personal and powerful, for in seeing those we know, we see ourselves, most especially if it's in the reflection of a window.

That was where Cratchit observed his fellow-lender Jack Dawkins[4], reduced to begging in these hard times. No

---

[4] Jack Dawkins.

Editor's note: The inclusion of Jack Dawkins brought about one of the first arguments between Dickens and his publisher. Dawkins had been a character in Dickens's second great success, Oliver Twist, however he was usually referred to differently. "Dear Charlie, If you keep calling the character by a name few readers will remember, they will have no idea who you're referring to. Please change back," the publisher wrote. However, Dickens vehemently refused. "I don't know what caused me to think of that silly nickname in the first place, which I was then stuck with. The fellow has a name, a real name, just as all of God's men and women have on Earth, and I intend to give him the good fortune of finally using it." After much more dissenting communication, they reached a compromise, where Dickens agreed to use Jack Dawkins's more recognizable name later in this new story. In his private diary, however, publisher Joseph Bunderston, wrote, "Some compromise. He uses 'Jack Dawkins' 875 times, and the more than 27, the fellow seemed so much older than his years tonight, accosting passersby with his hand out until some morsels of coin were given. His small frame was hunched over, his coat turned up high at the collar hiding himself. It liked to break Cratchit's heart.

"What ho, young Dawkins," he called out.

"Oh! Mr. Cratchit, is it?" The young fellow awkwardly looked around. "I really must be off."

"Yes, yes, Christmas Eve and all, I understand," Cratchit nodded compassionately with a polite wink, "Here, Let me give you a little something for the holiday, my gift to you."

If you had a spoon, you could have knocked Mr. Dawkins over with it. Most any other kitchen utensil would have done the job, as well. "We may all be competitors," Cratchit said, "but we are brothers in the selfsame profession. And what benefits my brothers, does so to me, as well."

Leaving the astounded Dawkins to his cold holiday season made all the warmer now, Cratchit swiftly walked to his dinner. Mr. Pickwick was right, he thought, times must be very tight.

(cont'd) other name I wanted – once." Scholarship shows this to be an exaggeration. Dickens only used the name 'Dawkins' 33 times. And he used the better-known nickname twice, albeit in the same paragraph, an occurrence most scholars likely believe to spite the publisher.

In any early evening, the <u>George and Vulture</u>[5] was a most convivial place. But on this Christmas Eve night, crowded with revelers preparing for the big day on the morrow, the tavern gave an air of camaraderie as never was.

With his family already upon their richly-deserved vacation, Bob Cratchit feasted on a hearty plateful of boiled mutton, boiled potatoes, boiled carrots, boiled beets, pickled herring and a boiling mug of Smoking Bishop. A lovely tankard it was, too, finely etched that put Bob in a wistful holiday mood, reminding him of an old, cherished silver mug his parents had had until it went sadly missing one Christmas Eve, a night like this one.

In reverie, Cratchit didn't notice at first the tall fellow who looked oddly lost, the rolled-up sleeves on his once-stylish coat a bit too long. At last, though, Bob caught the sport's eye. "I say, you look like you could use some company on a night like this, come and join me, sir."

---

[5] The George and Vulture.

From Dickens's notes: The following letter from Dickens was written to the proprietor of his favorite pub, the George and Vulture. "According to our contract when writing my Pickwick novel, you agreed to provide me with free drinks for the next seven years if I used the name of your establishment as that which Samuel Pickwick would patronize in the book. As our arrangement is now expiring, I would like to propose an extension, and if you are in agreement I will once again introduce the name of your pub, the George and Vulture, into my new story."

The man enthusiastically sidled over. "Kind of you. Very. Good wishes. Glad to share your evening. Very." Within moments, the two became the best of friends, and Alfred Jingle[6], for that was the stranger's name, toasted Bob's health and good wife. As Mr. Jingle had not yet dined, Cratchit called over a serving matron.

---

[6] Alfred Jingle.

Editor's note: When Dickens was set to turn in early pages of The Pickwick Papers, at the last minute he had the idea of a devilish cad of a ladies man, who he named Alfred Jingle. The character however was entered only rough form, with Dickens dropping in sample dialogue, leaving out most pronouns and occasional verbs, among other parts of speech. Upon receiving the pages, the publisher almost refused to release the chapters, calling it "amateurish" and "I didn't know what that Jingle person was saying most of the time." However, the publication deadline was at hand, and he was forced to go to press. As a result, Dickens himself had to stick with Jingle speaking in such a staccato style for the rest of the novel, something he felt mortified by, since he though it looked to readers like he didn't know how to write dialogue. When this new story came along, he proposed to the publisher that he bring back Mr. Jingle in order to finally get his dialogue right. Bunderston reluctantly agreed. Unfortunately, Dickens forgot about this until the last moment, at which point he was required to rush out the dialogue for the character, once again in the very same disjoined style.

"'Ere, love, my name is <u>Nancy</u>[7], I'll be your barmaid."
She looked askance at Jingle. "'Ello, you look thin as a rail,
you do. What's your pleasure?"

A lemon slice and crust of bread was all that Jingle
ordered. But Bob wouldn't hear of this. "You must be
starving," he exclaimed.

"And bloody poor, I'd say," the barmaid sneered.
"'Ere, I'll sneak you a piece of fish, I will. It ain't much, but
it's Christmas."

Bob's heart swelled by the crude thoughtfulness of

---

[7] Nancy.

Editor's note: Dickens was much taken by the character of
the dishonest but goodhearted barmaid with loose morals
when he created Nancy for the novel, <u>Oliver Twist</u>. In fact,
he loved the character so much that he came up with the
idea of writing a series of "Nancy" books. Dickens included
her in this story to be a showcase for the first of those
(tentatively titled, <u>Nancy and the Bullfighter</u>), to see how
the public would respond. When Bunderston read the
passages, however, he not only was taken aback at the idea,
suggesting that a series on the madcap romps of a
prostitute across Europe was not Dickens's most
substantive, no matter how "goodhearted" the character
was, but also reminded Dickens that the author had actually
killed off Nancy in the novel. As a result, Dickens reluctantly
dropped the plan and said her miraculous reappearance in
this new tale rising from the dead was instead to be
explained away to the public as an "homage."

this young woman who probably could hardly afford it herself. In its stead, he insisted on treating his new friend to a full banquet. "And there'll be quite a nice something extra left for you under the plate, my dear," he added with a wink to Nancy.

And so the spread arrived, plate by plate, bowl by bowl, dish by dish. "And a Smoking Bishop for my friend," Bob shouted out, "before you can say Jack Be Nimble."

At this, Jingle's face fell, for much as he appreciated the feast, he had his limits, and Smoking Bishop was on the other side of that line. He starred into the goblet for the longest time, but finally managed the tiniest sips of the orange, clove, grapefruit, sugar, and scalding wine and port mixture, his face cringing mightily at each ghastly drop.

"All of it, all the way, no sips, my good man, enjoy!" Bob burst forth with a jubilant whoop. "Drink for the season, full to the bottom!"

As Jingle was struggled with his drink, Cratchit spotted an old acquaintance. Who was it but none other than Old Mister Scrooge's former fiancé, Belle. Though She and old Scrooge had grown apart for decades, they had happily struck up again their friendship in his last years upon his renaissance. It was a solace to them both, and Bob Cratchit had been honored to observe how friendship is never lost, ever.

He embraced the grande dame in a hug that would like to have smothered a bear. "Bless my soul, Belle," he said, "How wonderful to see you on this night of nights."

"And you," she replied with surprising reserve, given the joviality of the room.

Finding himself between his two friends (Jingle still barely sipping at the drink), Cratchit suddenly leapt up. "My manners! Bless me, two dear friends and not an introduction amongst them!" With all his enthusiasm, Bob happily corrected the omission, nodding to each with a proud smile. "Jingle – Belle. Jingle – Belle." And then admonishing the unfinished beverage, "Jingle, all the way!"

Effusive as always in his questions, the lady provided polite, though curt replies. Yes, her dear husband passed on three years ago. Yes, her lovely daughter recently got married, goes by the name Copperfield now. Yes, it's a good Christmas. Yes, yes, yes.

"I am so very pleased to know that all is so well with you, Belle, and that you and your wonderful family are prospering so. Very, very pleased indeed."

Belle did not reply at first, keeping her composure. At length though she became moved to speak.

"'So well,' you say, Mr. Cratchit? I have held my tongue out of gentility, respect for dear Mr. Scrooge, and consideration to the season. But you try my patience."

If ever Bob had known what it was to bluster, it would have been now. Not a word could emit from his mouth. Certainly there must be some misunderstanding.

Alas, there was no misunderstanding. The tale Belle told was as clear as the tip of your nose on a summer's day, when nose tips are at their clearest. Several years back, Mr. Scrooge had so kindly set up a wonderful annuity for her through investments. The resources lay unneeded, but provided a comfort of security. With a granddaughter due in but months hence, it was finally time to partake of Mr. Scrooge's foresight.

"But when my son-in-law David ventured to our bank only last week, we found that our assets tied to Scrooge and Marley's had all recently been squandered, the investments shifted to charitable accounts of great risk, and all my protections gone. In short, sir, I now face a future most tenuous, at a time in my life when the recourses I have are painfully limited. As for your good wishes, I can only say but – bah, humbug."

What Bob hoped to explain was that these charity bond notes were no real risk at all, but something good, from which all men profit – if not always in pounds sterling, then in the sterling pounding of one's heart. Alas, since Belle had long since swept out of the tavern, explaining this to a chair would not have gotten its point across as effectively.

Left alone with Mr. Jingle, Cratchit was determined to show that his actions were truly as good as his word, and so Bob insisted on aiding his new, but poor friend beyond a mere supper. Layering Jingle's reticent hand with currency, and then emptying his wallet with the promised (and most-generous!) gratuity for the good-souled barmaid, Bob sat back far more full of heart now than even his meal had made him.

Cratchit's walk home was felicitous. His step light across the icy path. All about, it was beginning to look a lot like Christmas, everywhere he went. The sweet smells of fresh-baked Yuletide cakes and chestnuts roasting on an open fire. He bought several to warm his journey home, but passed the remainder to a little drummer boy beating out a joyful, yet incessant holiday rhythm. Shouts of "Have yourself a merry little Christmas" and "Blimey, if only I'd worn another sweater" cut into the frosty air. It was all such a beautiful sight, he was happy tonight, walking in a winter wonderland.

Turning down an alley, Cratchit thought he heard heavy steps behind him, when a large shadow loomed from the light of a gas streetlamp. To most men, the sight of <u>Bill Sikes</u>[8]

---

[8] Bill Sikes.

From the publisher's notes: "Dear Charlie, I know you said

beating a lead pipe into his calloused hand was one they hoped to see only in daylight, on open ground, at a distance of 500 paces, with a fence between them. And in the custody of the police, and preferably dead. To the ruffian himself, such impediments were mere distractions, except if he were dead, and even that not everyone was sure of.

"Mr. Sikes! What a pleasure to see you this fine eve of

(cont'd) not to intrude on this because you had a 'wonderful idea' for the character of a street tough in the story. But I had an insistent thought for a like character as Bill Sikes again, who was such an effective evil thug in <u>Oliver Twist</u>." When Dickens received this note, he misread it and thought that the publisher was saying he "liked" Bill Sikes and was "insisting" Dickens write the same character "again." Bothered, but not wishing to argue with a compliment, he decided it would be simpler to satisfy the request and fight larger battles another time, much to his annoyance later upon discovering the mistake. Afterwards, the publisher wrote to one of his partners that he had later received a letter from Dickens, "which tried to seem so jovial on the surface, but was blatantly curt, saying he would be giving free lessons in syntax so that any British schoolchild could learn where to place such words as 'like' properly in a sentence." Bunderston laughed it off, noting "That's why he's a writer, and I'm not," though clearly he felt hurt, since he added, "I'm just a publisher who pays him."

all eves," Bob smiled. "Are you doing last minute holiday shopping?"

Sikes angled his quarry against the wall. "The only shopping I be doing tonight, Cratchit, is for my employer to get th' money 'e is owed. There be concern you might leave the city afore it come due, now that you just happen to done sent your family off."

"A deserved rest from the winter's fury for such fine people, that's all. But for me, London is where I am. Leave? At Christmas time?! Perish the thought. It won't happen in this here parish. Ha, ha. Indeed, it is from our hearts where all men…"

"And it's from our wallets where we pays our debts." He yanked out Bob's billfold, which was empty as a water bucket in the Sahara. The ruffian threw it to the ground in disgust. "Not a good sign, at all. You just remember to pay up. One week."

With a shove, Sikes vanished into the fog. That's so like some people, Bob thought. Always rushing even during the holidays, and before I had a chance to wish him of the season. He sighed and headed home, as Christmas was waiting.

Now, it is a well-accepted fact, as opinions go, that a knocker on a door is the one part of a house where function is the sole duty over art. It knocks. It makes its sound. Bob Cratchit knows this. He knows it as well as he knows the back of his hand, and he knows the back of his hand as well as he knows the nose on his face. So why is it, I ask, that on this night, did Cratchit look at the knocker on his door and react with a start? For where a good, solid, plain English brass knocker should be, there was Scrooge's face.

Scrooge's face on his door knocker.

What in heaven's name was I thinking, thought Bob? In the month after Mr. Scrooge had passed on, Cratchit knew he wanted to honor his old benefactor, so he had replaced the original door knocker with one of Scrooge's likeness. What a foolish thing to have done, Cratchit admonished himself. Mr. Scrooge's head on my door? To pound against wood every single day? That is not how you honor someone. Yet, over the years, because it was but a knocker, it went unheeded. Until this very night of Christmas Eve.

"Bless my soul, I must replace that after the holidays," Cratchit said out loud.

Inside, he got a good fire going and was once more at peace, the old Bob. It was a large old house that had belonged to Mr. Scrooge, and before him Mr. Marley. When Scrooge died, Cratchit had bought the house from Fred, after the nephew put it on the market to buy a sailboat. It was a good house, and now it was his house.

It was also an empty house, as all the other Cratchits were on holiday in Scotland, in the Trossachs, getting the brisk air, relaxation and oat dishes. His dear wife looked forward to these trips each year, after so many years of deprivation, and everyone was disappointed that Bob didn't come along, though not so disappointed as to stay at home themselves. But he never liked leaving London at Christmastime, so much charity to give out, and besides he felt he just couldn't look at another plate of Yuletide haggis.

Although alone, he still decorated the house for the festivities. With a rum toddy, he sat in the library and sang Christmas carols, though he generally didn't know the words, so he hummed a good deal of the time. "Away in the manger la la la la la..." "Good King Wenceslas la la, at the feet of Stephen."

At last, a weary Bob Cratchit trod up the staircase. He

24

prepared himself for the night and lay in bed peacefully, saying his prayers, the first one as always being, "Please let me remember to say my prayers." As the wind swirled outside, the quiet of the house settled in, the only sound a distant chirp of a cricket on the hearth. All was calm. All was dark.

Then suddenly, a silver bell began to chime in the sitting room. And even more bells rang wildly through the house. It made such a clatter that Bob sprang from the bed to see what was the matter. He raced to the balustrade, and saw below that all through the house, a mouse was stirring, racing around and knocking into all the chimes. Eventually, the frightened creature left through the hole from which it had come. The bells ceased, and Cratchit returned to his four-poster, locking his door again behind him.

But before his head hit the pillow, he heard it. Coming up the stairs, a heavy clanging that scraped along the floor. Bob had risen in bed the moment he first heard the sounds. What was this terrible noise?? He just stared, frozen in his spot. And then outside his room, it stopped. It was as if Bob's heart stopped, as well. He could hear his own heart pounding, so clearly it hadn't stopped, and that was good news.

The door began to shake. And rattle violently. And shake some more!

"Humbug! Can someone open this door?!! It's locked. Bah."

"Mr. Scrooge??" The voice was his. Cratchit leapt to the door, unlocked it, and there in the doorway – was none other than his dear old friend Ebenezer Scrooge! Not Mr. Scrooge as he once was, but a Spectre, a gossamer apparition of the same.

"Bless my soul! Mr. Scrooge, come in."

"I'd have like to have come in earlier, if I didn't have

to stand around waiting for you to let me in," he snarled in the old way that was the old Mr. Scrooge which Bob remembered oh so well.

"Why didn't you just walk through the door? You are a ghost, are you not?"

Scrooge stood there for a moment. He slapped his head, feeling a fool. "Humbug! This is my first time at appearing-on-earth. It just slipped through my mind. That's what happens when you're old, you forget. You know how I spend my time these days? Looking for things I've misplaced. The Golden Years, bah!"

"Surely your existence can't be like that."

"You don't believe me?" Scrooge asked, his voice rising. His pale colour turning a lighter tone of pale.

"I don't."

"I come down to earth just for you, materialize in human form, and you suggest that I am lying? Lying??!"

"It's just that when one considers the majesty of afterlife, one must…"

"Oh, woe is me!" A mournful cry emitted from Scrooge's shaking soul. "My former junior partner who I viewed as almost a son thinks I went to the hereafter to become a liar. Kill me now, except that I'm already dead. Oh, woe is me!!"

"Mercy, Mr. Scrooge." Cratchit fell to his knees, his body shaking. "You would not say it and be upset if it were not so."

"That's more like it," snapped Scrooge instantly, back to his old self surprisingly quickly.

Yet unlike his old self, he now wore a long and heavy chain about his neck. Link by hideous link with oppressive amulets. Cratchit was affected by what he saw, that his beloved mentor, who had become as good a man as there was in this good old world, was still burdened by his former sins.

"The chain you forged in life," Cratchit whispered under his breath almost. "Oh, how I wish it were otherwise."

"What? This?" Scrooge looked confused. "No, this is a necklace I like. I never cared for jewelry during my life. But now, it's quite nice, don't you think?"

Cratchit quickly agreed, that it made him look quite dashing indeed. Scrooge's vanity was pleased by the compliment.

"It is so good to see you, Mr. Scrooge. And on tonight of all nights. I've missed your friendship, your kindness."

"You have missed my guidance, sir. You have sorely missed my skills. My knowledge. My talent. Leadership. Common sense."

"Mr. Scrooge?"
"You have missed my ability to add, subtract, multiply and divide. You have destroyed my life's work and in doing so done far worse than you can know!"

The rage of an apparition is that of the torrents of heaven crashed down upon earth. Scrooge's wrath was the wrath of a wraith. So frightening was it that Cratchit would have been described as trembling in his very boots, but that he only had on one slipper. So, he trembled in his slipper.

"But Mr. Scrooge," he weakly croaked, "I am a good proprietor. I have done your legacy proud." As he spoke, Cratchit's own spirit grew while facing the spirit before him.

"Bless my soul, I walk in full comfort for the charity I have provided the helpless and those in want of saving. I defy any man and former man to say elsewise. I have succeeded in my work, in my company, in my life. Mankind is my business."

"No!" Scrooge bellowed. "Business is kind, man! Prosperity is kind. Enterprise, industriousness, planning are kind. Investments, that's the kind of saving you should be practicing! All of my efforts to edify you, sir, have been in vain, and I suffer in seeing the result. Your mismanagement has thrown away treasured resources until they can do no good evermore. Without a foundation, you have cast away the future into darkness!"

If Bob Cratchit had had a moment of fortitude, that was now but a long-distant memory. Quaking before Mr. Scrooge, he steadied himself the best he could which wasn't very steady.

"Hear me, now!" spoke Scrooge, an intensity in his voice not usually attributed to wispy phantoms. "You have a chance to change. A chance to be the man you can become. Heed my words."

"I will, Ebenezer. Thank you."

"I wasn't finished," Scrooge replied with a certain petulance. "You will be visited by three Spirits, each at the stroke of one. All of them tonight. Yet separately. It's complicated, I know, but you have to trust me on this."

"That is a bit inconvenient, Mr. Scrooge, tomorrow being Christmas and all," said Bob hesitantly, for he had but little experience discussing such matters with an Apparition. "Might they perhaps put off the visits until after the holiday season? Any time in January would be most fine."

"Expect the first Spirit tonight." Scrooge looked at Cratchit with a ghostly pallor, an understandable demeanor all things considered. "Hither lies the fate that has befallen others."

Leaning halfway out the window into the brutal night, Scrooge pulled Cratchit forward with him. Bob thought this less than a wise act, and if it was the sort of judgment that phantoms had, perhaps this three visits idea might not be such a good one.

Images floated in the hazy atmosphere across the darkened sky. Bodies of tattered men drifted past, shooting stars fell like loose beads, a reindeer with a red nose flew by. There was a cacophony of sounds intermingled – an anguished requiem of singing, laughter and cries – one noise quite indistinguishable from the next, though "Quit playing that bloody organ, some people are trying to sleep" came through reasonably clearly.

So transfixed was Cratchit that he didn't notice that Scrooge had vanished. Left alone in the room, he trundled back to bed in his one slipper. Tucked safely again under his quilt, Bob began to wonder if he truly had experienced what he imagined.

"Bless my soul," he said aloud to no one, not counting himself. "It is not a good idea to mix one's libations. Oh, my, what a stir I have given myself." The thought of this put him in mind to make another hot rum toddy, just to calm himself, of course, and so he put on a dressing gown and hobbled down the stairs in his slipper.

Seated in the library, Cratchit refilled his beverage, feeling ever so much more relaxed. A flame danced on a candlestick, throwing eerie shadows on the wall. Oooo, he thought, ghosts, and laughed. And how many flames can dance on the head of a candlestick, he thought, too, and chortled once again. Not that any of this was especially funny, but it was Christmas, the time of jolly gatherings and lively good will, and several libations.

Just then, the clock struck one.

Stave Two

THE FIRST OF THE
THREE SPIRITS ARRIVES

C ratchit apprehensively leaned forward in his chair when the clock struck one, and he waited for the Spirits of which he had been foretold.

At twenty minutes past, however, no Spirit had arrived. "I expected not," thought an exhausted Bob, and then half-asleep padded over to make a late-night snack while keeping his vigil. With a plate of Stilton, he sipped his snifter of port, comforted in knowing that he was alone and that the spirits in his glass were the only ones that would be appearing tonight.

Suddenly, a wrathful voice pierced through the house.

"Is anybody here?! I've been waiting for half an hour!

Bob Cratchit liked to freeze in his chair, his body colder than when leaning out the window with Scrooge, though at least now there was no risk of plummeting two stories to the ground. That voice! It was coming from upstairs in his bedroom. And was like no voice Cratchit had ever heard, ethereal yet very much of this earth.

"And a little light would be nice, thank you very much. Hallo?! I'm only waiting ten more minutes. Fifteen at the most."

Cratchit carefully made his way up the stairs. Could this be the Spirit of which Scrooge had spoken? It must be. His candle shined into his room, and he could see a shadow in the corner, looking as if it were tapping its foot in impatience.

"There you are," Cratchit heard. "It's about time. Some people are more polite with their guests. Others think about more than themselves. Tush."

Bob saw the figure, as close to Cratchit as I am to you, and I am about eighteen inches from you, unless you are nearsighted, in which case perhaps two feet. Translucent like a wraith, to be sure, yet of this earth. The Spectre looked to be a very old shriveled man, having a hard face of many trials thickly covered with matted red hair. He was dressed in a dingy, thick flannel coat that dropped down to his ankles and had an angry way about him, although being eternally dead has that effect on some.

"Are you the Spirit whose presence was foretold to me?" Cratchit inquired.

"Probably," it answered. "But as I wasn't here when you were foretold, that would be hard to swear to, now wouldn't it?"

32

"What is your purpose here, Spirit?"

The Apparition looked Cratchit up and down. "Are you aware that you're only wearing one slipper?"

"There are powers in the world far beyond my purview, Spirit. I know not yet what I have to learn."

"I am here to show you Christmas Past."

"My past?"

The visitor did not speak for a moment. Then, "No, your next-door neighbor's," it sneered. "We thought he was much more interesting."

"Oh, Ghost of Christmas Past, there is a world of…"

"I am not the 'Ghost of Christmas Past.'" the Spectre interrupted. "I didn't even want to be here. And I waste a half hour waiting for you to show up." He began pacing about the room, slowly at first, soon though with more force, rolling his fingers angrily. "No one wanted to be here! It's Christmas Eve. Who wants to go out on Christmas Eve? But they send me. 'You go, Fagin[9],' they say. Why? Why me, I ask?" And

---

[9] Fagin.

Editor's note: Dickens had come under some criticism for the character of Fagin in <u>Oliver Twist</u>. There were those who felt the portrayal of the malicious leader of young boy pickpockets bordered on anti-Semitic. Dickens felt the rebukes to be very unfair, and in one well-reported argument at a dinner party with the wife of a Jewish friend, he avowed he had no idea where anyone would even ever

here he quickly spun back to Cratchit. "It's because I'm Jewish! To my face they say it. 'It's Christmas Eve, Fagin, is it fair to send the others? You go, it's not your holiday. We'll send the Ghost of Christmas Past to one of your people's homes on Hanukkah.'"

Cratchit didn't want to upset a Spirit, although the situation was clearly far past that point already. He settled on expressing his regret that his guest had to come tonight, and politely said how it showed what good cheer and kindness he had within him.

"Everyone gets Christmas off," Fagin continued, still

(cont'd) get the idea. It was pointed out to him that it might be because he referred to Fagin as "The Jew" on about every third page. "Oh, that," he famously replied. "I thought that was poetic license." He continued to make the case that it truly was never his intent to be hurtful, noting that he had written significantly worse villains and no one said he was anti-Episcopalian just because he created Bill Sikes who was a terrorizing brutal murderer, or Quilp, a character hideously more venal than Fagin who even drives a little girl to her death. When it was explained to Dickens that he never once referred to either character as "Episcopalian," he is reported to have slapped himself in the head and responded, "I didn't?! Oy, as the Jews wisely say. I meant to." Embarrassed, Dickens vowed to make up for the wrong perception of Fagin, and made the decision to bring the character back in this story and let him speak for himself.

spewing. "I like a holiday as much as the next soul."

"Ghost of Christmas Pa..." Cratchit quickly corrected himself, as the Wraith snapped an angry look to him, "*Fagin.* I can only but say that you and I shall make the merriest Christmas together. Indeed, sir, it is the delight in our hearts, rather than possessions, that connects us all."

"Ach, you say that now, because you're young," said Fagin, who then looked Cratchit up and down. "Or reasonably young. But when you're old and it's cold, and who cares if you live or you die, the one consolation's the money you may have put by."

"I can never believe that, Spirit. But I know you are here to be my guide for things which may be unknown to me. So, lead on, Spirit, lead on."

Fagin pressed Cratchit to follow and floated outside. Bob peered into the abyss. He wondered why Spirits were so intent on always going out windows, when there was a perfectly good door on the ground floor. "I am mortal and could fall," he whimpered.

"If you fall, you fall," Fagin shrugged. "That's a chance you take. If you fall, my job is over, and I can go back."

Cratchit looked on with horror.

"Tush, tush," continued Fagin with a sarcastic laugh. "Do you think they had me come all the way here so you could fall?? Such a fool they sent me to. Touch my hand."

As the ancient Spirit wafted into the sky, Cratchit took a careful step after. Suddenly, his hand slipped from Fagin's, and his heart pounded as he believed himself about to plummet. But just as instantly, Fagin took hold of Cratchit's fingers.

"Haha! Tricked you!" the Spectre chortled. "I would wager that gave you the fright of a death of Sundays. Thought you would face eternity. How was it? Ha ha."

As much as Bob wanted to answer in as colorful terms as could be mustered, he felt it the wisest course to remain silent when you are being supported high up in the firmament by a spectral being.

When Cratchit felt his feet touch the blessèd terra firma, he peeled open his eyes to a world of enchantment. He and his new friend stood on a lush veldt, the deep green grasses swaying at their waists. Turning, he leapt with unbridled fear, for thundering at him were the largest and strangest-looking creatures he would ever see. A Tyrannosaurus Rex crushed after what could only be a Triceratops. Only one hundred yards away now. And now, but fifty. Nearer, almost upon them.

"Fagin!!" Cratchit called out, barely able to find his voice.

"I'm sorry. I must have taken you back too far into the past. Here we go."

And just as the Olympian dinosaurs were close enough for Bob to feel the wind of their moving force, he and the Spirit blended away and found themselves in safety, back in England once more.

"How's that? Better?" Fagin inquired.

Bob collapsed to touch the verdant meadow of a village square, each blade a tender testament to hospitality and home.

"Do you recognize that schoolhouse" the old Wraith

added.

Bob looked down the long, winding dirt path, lined by snow-covered mulberry bushes enlivening the way. At the far end stood a one-room building of hearty wood.

He turned to Fagin. "No. I've never seen it in my life."

"Take a closer look." Fagin motioned slyly. "Come. Several young ones await."

Man and Spirit headed through the village and came upon a playground by the school. Laughter burst forth, as two boys and a little girl, bundled in heavy winter muffs, were engaged in a game of Sticks and Bones. Fagin stood to the side, a knowing look upon his face. Bob smiled, as well, their youthful innocence a joy to see.

"Who are they?" he asked.

"Oh, surely you recognize them. You must."

Cratchit could only shrug his shoulders and shake his head.

"I know it's been a long time, but honestly. Try again." But there was no reason to, for indeed they were strangers unknown to Bob. The old Spectre started kicking at the ground at this turn of events. However there was little he could do about the mistake. The past is past, even if you are the Ghost of Christmas Past, or just standing in for him.

"All right, all right. Sue me. All English villages look the same. Once more." Fagin yanked Cratchit by his coat, and the scene faded to another country neighborhood. They were in a narrow street, snow layering the ground. Fagin abruptly pointed to one of the cottages, latticed brown and white, with smoke coming from the chimney.

"There. Do you recognize *that*??"

"My childhood home!"

Fagin breathed a deep sigh of relief and looked heavenward, throwing his hands outward . "Thanks God." Then, "Do you know the way?"

"Know it?! I could walk it blindfolded."

"Oh, you can, can you? Trying to show off a little, maybe? All right, let's see." He handed his scarf to Cratchit. At first, Bob wasn't sure this was serious, but as Fagin kept waving his hand at him, he tied the garment around his eyes. "Let's go."

Cratchit did a respectable job upon his initial steps. Soon though, he bumped into a tree, stumbled through some shrubbery, and became completely disoriented.

"It's not so easy as you think, is it?" Fagin said, holding his hand out impatiently for Bob to return the muffler. "My way is easier, no? Shall we?"

Cratchit stood, but even before he reached Fagin the scene had faded, and they were inside the very same house.

A menagerie of children ran around the parlour playing Jacks in Seven, making up the rules as they went along for no one precisely knew the game. The house was one of gentle ease. Not mighty wealth, no, but a place where all needs were met and no one wanted for want. Happy children, happy faces, happy hearth, happy times.

Happy Bob as he stood with Fagin and watched. A single tear rolled down his cheek. "So good to remember such goodness from a distance long past. Such comfort."

"Comfort is good, then? Being comfortable."

With that a cheer went up as a woman older than the rest, but younger in spirit – "spirit," that is, as in feeling, not "Spirit" like a ghost – entered the room wiping her hands on an apron. "Now, you little children make sure you don't ruin your big appetites, for Christmas goose is on the way."

"A Christmas goose, mother, a Christmas goose," the shout went up from Thomas and William, the latter of whom, a year younger than his twelve-year-old brother, always insisted on being louder.

"Oh, mother, it will be the most wonderful Christmas ever," sang Mary, the eldest of the clan, not counting her parents.

"As I live and breathe it will, when your father and Little Bob get home," replied Mother Cratchit, a sweet-tempered woman with brown hair tied in a bun. "You watch the wee 'uns in the meantime," she nodded to a boy and two girls playing a game of Staring Ever Staring. Such were the burdens for Mary being eighteen and at the age of responsibility, but it was no burden to her, for she loved them all, and she loved most especially that their favorite game was to glare in silence at one another for hours at a time.

"Oh, Spirit, I remember this sad Christmas," Bob said, his voice lowering. "The year my father took me to his office."

"At least you got to spend Christmas with people you expected to," Fagin muttered under his breath. "And didn't have to drag some total stranger around."

"What?"

"Nothing. Never mind. Pay attention."

As Mother Cratchit brought out the Christmas goose, and the children helped with all the trimmings, shouting cheers of joy, the front door opened, and John Cratchit entered, followed by a little boy who walked with a limp and hobbled into the parlour.

"Oh, Little Bob, whatever is the matter?" called out Mother Cratchit, running to the boy.

"Father was angry, kicking at the ground, kicking at trees, and I got in the way by accident," the youngster sheepishly answered, rubbing his shins.

John Cratchit was a hearty man with raggedy hair, raggedy beard and an affable smile, which was working back up to its good old self. He took his wife aside to whisper.

"What? What's he saying?" Fagin asked Bob, cupping his ear. "Why doesn't he speak up?" He yelled over, "Speak up, man! We didn't come here for our health."

Cratchit explained that father was saying a note had been tacked upon on his place of employ, announcing that the business was closing, and he was out of work.

"But a happy Christmas we shall have, for all Christmas is ever happy!" the father called out effusively.

"Whatever shall we do for money, though, John?" Mother Cratchit asked with a worried air. "We owe such as it is and have but few savings."

"Bless my soul, then we shall find ways," her husband replied with a reassuring voice. "If we needs sell our dearest household items, be thankful we have them to sell."

Fagin gave Bob a nudge in the ribs, making sure Cratchit heard this last sentence. "Eh?" The other glared at the Ghost who looked back innocently, "I'm just saying."

John Cratchit gathered the family and explained that whatever travails they faced, they would always have each other.

"A sweet man," Bob sighed.

"Indeed," Fagin agreed. "Of course, if he still had a job, they'd have each other and money, too. But then, that's just the way my mind works."

"Selling what we had helped, but we had less than we thought," replied Bob, not hearing him, or pretending not to. He pointed around the room. "That gravy boat there was worth but little, some valuable antique china got broken, this silver mug was so dearly valuable but somehow got misplaced …" his voice trailed off, as he recalled the goblet at the George and Vulture earlier tonight, though in the future, whenever it was. "That would have helped pay the rent. It all would have helped."

The Spectre looked at him a brief moment. "Are you going to kvetch the rest of the time we're together? Because if you are, I've got plenty of complaints of my own. To start with, I'm dead."

The family gathered around the Christmas table, and what a feast it was, to lift their hopes! Christmas goose enough to feed a kingdom. Three French hens and two turtle doves roasted to a luscious crisp, even a partridge smothered with pear sauce for the wee 'uns. John Cratchit led his family in festive song. "Hark, the happy angels sing," his enthusiasm soared, for joy is often more important than accuracy. Mrs. Cratchit told a raucous story about the parish priest and a donkey. And Little Bob stood on his chair to solemnly remind all Who it was they were celebrating the day for.

"Nothing like bringing a party to a halt, is there," noted Fagin. "Quite a little pisher you were, eh?"

"It was the best of times," Bob stated, watching his memory before him, "and the worst of times. If only we'd been able to sustain ourselves just a bit more. We didn't need much. How our lives changed soon after."

"They would have made that much of a difference? Simple possessions, a mere silver mug was that valuable?" Fagin asked pointedly.

"Oh, my, yes, some things would have been of extreme worth, near priceless."

Fagin nodded with a thoughtful sway of his head. "Wait, look!" He suddenly pointed into the hallway. "Over there!"

"What?!"

As Cratchit looked away, Fagin quickly grabbed the silver mug off the shelf and hid it in the deep pocket of his coat. "My mistake, I thought I saw something," he said and then took Cratchit by the arm. "Come. We have another Christmas."

The two swept through the room. As they passed by the dining room table, Fagin's sleeve accidentally knocked several pieces of exquisite imported china off the table, and they shattered.

The image of the table faded into a more intimate one. Bob saw another vision of himself, dining with a young woman. The tearoom was lovely, but not so lovely as the girl. A bit dim (the establishment, that is), it was full of patrons enjoying the high life. <u>Amy Dorritt</u>[10] was a sparkle all herself, little she was, but with a big vivaciousness that reflected in young Robert Cratchit's eyes. Her fiancé (for that is what Cratchit was) rejoiced that he was the richest man in the world in every possible way, except for money.

"These prices do appear a bit dear, dear," he noted while uncomfortably scanning the menu and pulling at his tattered coat sleeve.

"Oh, Robert, it's Christmas, I care only for our holiday together." Little Dorrit replied as they waited to be joined by another couple. "If your clothes have holes, it is the man that fills them that matters. Though if you could cover up that one here in your pants, it might be nice."

---

[10] Amy Dorritt.

From Dickens's notes: "Naming a character Tiny Tim seemed to work so well in A Christmas Carol. The public reacted far more enthusiastically than I ever imagined for a character who is so deeply uninteresting and treacly. All I can imagine is that the apparently adorable, diminutive quirk to his name must have made him so endearing to readers. I shall try it again with Amy Dorritt, but also call her Little Dorritt, in the same way. Let us see if lightning does indeed strike a second time in the identical place." He later expanded on the character when he wrote the novel, <u>Little Dorritt</u>, and once more looked for lightning to strike a second time by returning exactly to his roots of <u>Oliver Twist</u>, placing the virtuous and ever-sweet young girl again in a workhouse, though disguising it only slightly as a debtor's prison.

Cratchit turned to Fagin, feeling a need to explain. "Times had been so very hard for my family back then. Dear Amy made me feel good about what really mattered."

"Everything I know about women can be put on this grain of salt," the Wraith responded. "And even I know that that polite, elegant girl is mortified."

Just then, the other couple entered the room, and a handsome couple they were. The young woman was striking with full blond hair flowing down her back, and an air of petulance that every eye in the room was not on her. The man had a dashing way about him, with a piercing look of insouciance, a rare combination indeed.

"Oh, Amy sweet, I have the most grand news," the arriving young woman said. "Mr. Carton and I have become as one. We are married!"

Well, there was such a shout of joy from Amy. She hugged Estella[11] and cried and hugged her once more, Estella

---

[11] Estella.

From the publisher's notes: "Dear Charles, I've noticed that in all your stories, they are populated with young women who are all virtuous, ever-sweet, pure, and the heaven's epitome of goodness. Might it not be interesting to try for once, please, to have a young girl who was perhaps more normal?" Dickens had heard this complaint elsewhere, so he tried this suggestion with Estella. For contractual reasons, he was also required to bring the character back in a novel, which he did more fully in Great Expectations as the beautiful, but selfish and coldly uncaring ward trained explaining that she simply couldn't have born not being Mrs. Sidney Carton[12] one day longer, and Cratchit said he wanted to

---

(cont'd) to be that way by the crazy Miss Havisham. However, he didn't care for writing a character like Estella and went back happily to writing virtuous, ever-sweet, and pure young women as he had before.

[12] Sidney Carton.

Editor's note: His whole career, Dickens was always looking for a catchphrase that would grab the public's fancy, which he could use for marketing purposes. He thought he'd come up with one in Tiny Tim's "God bless us, everyone," but that was considered by the courts as too generic and therefore in the public domain. He worked around a few ideas for this tale, but never thought he got it quite right. One struck his interest, though, which he kept fine-tuning and later felt it would perfectly fit a minor character from this Christmas story. For <u>A Tale of Two Cities</u>, therefore, Dickens expanded that character just so he could speak the catchphrase, and thus Sidney Carton made his full-fledged appearance, as a bored, ne'er-do-well, who finally has a moment of revelation on the last page (where Dickens felt it would be most dramatic and get the most attention) and blurts out, "It's a far, far better thing I do now than I have ever done before." The phrase caught on, Dickens licensed it often, and it was seen on such products as kites, a line of shaving products, garden rakes, and was embroidered on the backs of work shirts. One enterprising stage producer order a bottle of champagne to celebrate, adding since that option was beyond interest of his wallet, instead would raise his cup of good English tea to the happy couple.

Estella grew suddenly cold and looked down her pretty nose at the beverage and up that very same nose to Cratchit. Little Dorrit wasn't quite certain how to respond either, but at last joined him in his good wishes.

Fagin just stared at Cratchit, speechless, and could only slap himself on the forehead several times.

"What? What did I do?" asked Bob. "It's our national drink."

"I would say that I don't want to be seen with you, but happily no one can."

Meals were delivered, and the enthusiastic Mr. Carton began ravishing his sumptuous feast. Amy had shifted away, closer to Estella. Robert pushed aside his piece of mackerel tried to get Little Dorritt's attention, but her back was to him.

"It's a far, far better bowl of vichyssoise I eat now than I have ever eaten before," Mr. Carton cried out with relish. "Everything makes our celebration sweeter."

"So, do tell me, dear, where will you and Mr. Carton be going for your honeymoon? I must know," inquired Amy with wide-eyed curiosity.

Leaning in from his ostracized position, Robert was able to

(cont'd) bought the rights to help promote his latest play, and took out advertisements in newspapers with the star of the show using the quote, praising his own performance.

make out some of the conversation, though just barely.

"You know, Amy dear," Estella enthused, pointedly kissing her husband on the cheek, "I have asked Mr. Carton to take me to Paris; you must join us New Year's Eve."

"Oh, that would be ever so wonderful," said an excited Amy, bouncing out of her chair, until her eyes fell on Robert, his tattered clothes and even more tattered expression.

He whispered to her, "I really cannot afford such trips right now, Miss Dorrit. But you go."

"No, Robert, if my fiancé can't go, how I could possibly attend unescorted?" With a quivering voice, she said, "I'm sorry, Estella, I don't believe I'll be able to accept your offer."

Fagin scratched his head above his ear. "I must say, Cratchit, you do know how to show a girl a good time."

As Robert at the table shrunk in his seat, the older Bob shrunk at the memory, so vivid and painful once again.

Amy regained her composure with a cheerful voice, "Your nuptials suit you so well, Estella. Marriage sounds oh-so frightfully wonderful."

"It's a far, far better woman I have met now than I have ever met before," Sidney exploded, adding a kiss to Estella's cheek.

"Speaking of marriage, dear," Estella said to Amy, "You have been with your gentleman for ever the longest time."

"Almost ten months. He's a kind man."

"Indeed, he is. But what kind?" And the women laughed that rich, lively laugh that made Robert view the mackerel on his plate and think that it was the lucky one. Estella gave a look at Robert and turned back to Amy. "You and I must talk at lunch one day," and then she leaned in close, "soon."

"Now, I am not an expert," the Ghost said to Cratchit, putting a grandfatherly arm on his shoulder, "but my guess is that the next Christmas vision is not going to be a good one for you love birds."

"Spirit," said Bob tentatively, trying to figure out how to broach the subject, since he knew that Fagin's guess was all too accurate, "perhaps it would be possible to skip the next and jump instead to the shadows that follo…"

Cratchit saw that he was now standing in a parlour.

"Oh, too late, sorry!" Fagin reported. "If only you had spoken up sooner."

The room was elegant with expensive furnishings. Amy stood at a large window, looking out upon the snowy lawn, her eyes with tears. Sitting uncertainly nearby, the young Cratchit was older than before by a year – the very same as she.

"There is nothing more to say," Little Dorrit recounted, though she found it in her a way to say more. "Another Idol has displaced you. You are a good man, but no longer bring me the comfort I need."

"What Idol is it that has displaced me" he asked his dear girl.

"A golden one. Ever since my father regained his lost fortune, I have been accustomed to that way of life. Treasured as I hold you in my heart, I know my heart can just as easily treasure one with real treasures. I do not wish to return to poverty."

"We would never be poor with love amongst us," he replied. "It sustains all."

"You are but a scrivener."

"A most honorable job."

"Robert, dear – I don't even know what a scrivener is!"

The young man thought a moment, uncertain how best to describe it. "I copy text for good people of good deeds."

"That will never be enough for me. And shouldn't be for you. Copying others." The dear girl knelt before him. "As long as you are a scrivener in practice, you will be a scrivener at heart. I seek your release."

Looking on this from across the room with Fagin, Bob Cratchit nodded yes, as did his younger self. No matter how happy men may be, he now saw there can still be.

Fagin interrupted Bob's reveries. "Come, we must go."

"Your time grows short?"

"No, very late. I still am yet to eat, it's Christmas and I have friends to see."

Before Cratchit could answer, the scene faded to a small, barren flat. A figure knelt under a lone chair, searching for some token. Suddenly, this scene faded and they were in a counting-house.

"Wait!" Cratchit called out. "What was that?!"

"I thought you knew," replied the Ghost. "It's your life. Don't ask me."

"You went too fast. Wait, can we go back?"

"Sorry, we have to move on."

The counting-house was a cold place, dark and dank, and the only spirit in it was the one standing next to Bob.

"Do you recognize this place?" that Spirit asked.

"I was an apprentice here!"

As they entered a small room, Bob Cratchit saw his younger self working to the bone, a Christmas tree and decorations by his desk. He was new to the firm, having decided to get a real job that could provide benefits. And the first benefit had paid off, he was dating a wonderful girl, good-hearted, and able to treat her to small pleasures, income being a magical thing indeed. Though she loved Bob, she liked the treats, too, and it had help draw them even closer, giving them special things to enjoy together.

A reedy man, with a glower in one eye and a deeper glower in the other, tapped his foot impatiently and making an intentionally loud noise, hoping to be paid heed.

"Why it's Jacob Marley, alive again!" cried Cratchit the elder. "Bless my soul, as I live and breathe, so does he."

Cratchit exclaimed how good it was to see Marley, but thought it was best to see him from the distance of many decades knowing that he was long dead and that Cratchit was only there as a vision. In addition to reedy, Marley was flinty, stingy and nasty.

"O-ho, Bob! O-ho, Edwin!" Marley stamped.

The shadow of Cratchit's former self stepped into the main room, and around the corner came his fellow-apprentice.

"Edwin Drood[13], alive again, too!" shouted Cratchit with great joy. "Bless my soul, he was a nice lad, though a bit moody and mysterious. Still, we got along well."

"Why did you fall out of touch?" Fagin inquired.

"He got fired from the firm for some reason, and I don't know what happened to him after. I heard that he had signed on with a peg-legged sea captain to go hunt a white whale[14] in

---

[13] Edwin Drood.

Editor's note: When writing this book, Dickens came up with what he thought was his most brilliant idea ever for using the Edwin Drood character in his own story. He told friends it was full of mystery, suspense, social consciousness deeper than he'd ever done, incredible twists, uproarious comedy, stunning surprises, and heart-wrenching drama. He almost began the new "Drood novel" several times, but kept getting drawn away on other projects, and because he loved the idea so much, considering it superior to anything he'd yet written, he refused to work on it until he could give it his full attention. At last, he cleared his schedule and started writing The Mystery of Edwin Drood. Unfortunately, Dickens died halfway through and never completed it.

[14] White whale.

From the publisher's notes: "Dear Charles, I understand that your book here is a fantasy, but I believe you go much too far with your reference of a vengeful peg-leg captain

America for revenge, but that sounds absurd, doesn't it?"

As Marley put the money he was counting into a drawer, his partner joined him,

"Mr. Scrooge, alive again, also!" the elder Cratchit cried out.

"Yes, he's alive, they're all alive, we're in the past before they all died, I thought you had figured that out by now," the Ghost retorted, shaking his head.

The two owners addressed their apprentices, who quivered from the cold. The owners quivered, too, though that was a natural condition for them.

"What did I tell you two about Christmas decorations?!" Mr. Scrooge sneered.

"I believe you said it was a 'bedbug.'" Edwin replied, an

(cont'd) hunting a white whale. Do such colored leviathans even exist? Ghosts and Spirits are one thing, but whale hunting is earthbound, and a known and important industry which the public understands. Moreover, who in the world would fight a whale for revenge, even in their wrong mind? Your character asks if such a thing sounds absurd, and I answer that query with a hearty yes. It is most absurd!" As a result of publisher Bunderston's scathing comments, Dickens dropped plans for his next novel that would have delved into this whale story much deeper, very reluctantly agreeing to trust the publisher's business judgment. Eight years later, Herman Melville wrote <u>Moby Dick</u>. Dickens is reported to have been quite unhappy.

earnest look on his face. Young Cratchit had to control himself to keep from laughing.

"Though Mr. Cratchit may find this amusing, what Mr. Marley and I do not find amusing are the decorations you two have put up expressly against our wishes."

"It is for only one day a year, sir," said Bob, who tried in vain to look serious.

"That's no excuse for making our place of business look like a forest carnival," Marley snarled.

"So, if you want a Merry Christmas without 'bedbugs,'" spit out Scrooge whilst glaring at Drood, " and keep your positions, I suggest you make changes. Immediately."

It was remarkable how those two young fellows went at it. One, two, three, Bob took down several trees – four, five, six, Edwin gathered all the holly that decked the hall – seven, eight, nine, the men removed the nativity scene and piles of straw – ten, eleven, twelve, they tossed out frankincense and threw away the myrrh, which had been so difficult to find – thirteen, fourteen, fifteen, stopped to catch their breaths – sixteen, seventeen, eighteen and, also, nineteen – grabbed lawn elves, hauled down the wooden reindeer strung across rafters, hid the statue of Henry II they had dressed as St. Nicholas – and before you could say twenty – wait, no, first they swept up the pine needles spread everywhere – they collapsed before you could say Good King Wenceslas.

As this whirled on, Fagin wandered around the room, marveling at the fury of activity. His aimless direction took him to the counting desk. There, with the others distracted, the Spirit emptied the drawer of all the money therein, filling his pockets.

With the tinkle of a bell, the door to the firm opened, and a young woman stepped in. She was a sweet girl, with rosy cheeks, though that might have been due to the frigid temperatures outside. She inquired of Mr. Scrooge for Bob Cratchit.

The other Bob Cratchit, the one in shadows, had all of his being light up. "Bless my soul, it's my heart's beloved...!"

"I swear, if you say, 'Alive again!' I will haunt you forever," the Ghost snapped.

"I know this night. I know why she is here," Bob enthused excitedly, which as all the world knows is the finest of ways to enthuse. "Hush, hush, I want you to see this."

The woman in question was directed to the gentleman in question to the back room, with the admonition from Scrooge that time was money and she should be quick about it. She smiled politely, thanked him politely, nodded "the season to you" politely, and when Scrooge turned away with a "Humbug," she made a most unladylike gesture.

"Bob, dearest Bob, you asked me here. Forever why?" the sweetest lady inquired.

The young man dropped quickly to his knee. "My sweet dearest, now that I am a man with a salary, with a future – dearest of all dears who I could ever hold dear, will you be mine forever, my dear?"

At that very moment, the elder Bob Cratchit's attention was diverted as he saw the Ghost turn weak. "Your time!," he cried with concern, "Does it finally grow short?!"

"No, dear, it's not that, dear," Fagin snipped, "oh, no, the dearest and most dear dear that ever dearly was, not at all, my sweet dear." Finally, he got some gray back in his cheeks. "Come, man, have at least a touch of consideration for others within hearing distance. Show some mercy."

Old Cratchit noticed that the young woman had wiped away her tears of joy, and quickly he quieted his traveling companion. "Watch! Watch what she answers."

"She's your wife. I've figured out what she answers. Do you take me for a total schlemiel?"

At that moment, away in the front office, Scrooge's partner slammed a drawer, loud enough to wake the dead, present company excepted. It drew the two shadowed visitors' rapt attention. "Mr. Drood!" Marley shouted.

"Sir?"

"Not five minutes ago, this drawer was full of money, and now it is empty of that same money. Only one person has been by this drawer, and that one person is you."

"I know nothing of your money, Mr. Marley. So little of it have I seen anywise."

"I know you, sir, and your kind. Christmas Eve or no, you can take your thieving ways and sneering and go. You are fired!"

"Poor lad," the elder Bob said wistfully, as he watched Drood trudge out into the cold air and even colder life ahead. "So, that's what happened. I can't believe he took the money, but that Mr. Marley was looking for an excuse to release him."

"Yes, yes, that must be it," the Ghost coughed. "Yes."

Away from the excitement, the now-engaged couple was otherwise engaged and embracing. "Oh, my dear Bob who is so dear to the dearest of…"

"Oh, for goodness sake!" Fagin shouted. "Enough!" The vision swiftly changed, and they found themselves in the snowy street.

"Hold!" called Cratchit, "I wanted to see that. Why did you leave?"

"If I had to listen …" the Spirit stopped and rather than argue with a lovesick pup, he reached into his pocket and pulled out a timepiece which he shoved in Cratchit's face, "How about – 'My time grows short.' How's that? You seem to feel that's important." He bellowed theatrically, "My time grows short!"

An unhappy look crossed Cratchit's face. "That's my pocket watch."

"No, it isn't. I've had it for ages," Fagin shot back, perhaps too quickly.

"You took it from my bedroom!" Bob grabbed for the piece.

"My time draws near."

"Don't you leave me, we are not yet done discussing this!" Cratchit advanced on the Spirit, who was quicker than you would suppose for one so elderly and dead. Bob gave chase, down the cobbled high street they went. At length, the old Wraith stopped, no longer willing to continue dashing through the snow, and he faced the angry Cratchit.

"Wait, don't you see," Fagin squawked. "It worked! What I intended all along. This watch, it's just…metal, glass." He was thinking fast on his feet now. "What is a watch, eh? If you drop it, does it not dent? If you throw it, does it not break? It has no heart, no soul, yet now you see that even a simple possession has value, eh? Value enough to drive a man to a frenzy to possess it!"

Cratchit stood transfixed, a sense of uncertainty. "Yes, there is something in what you say." The Ghost heaved a sigh of relief. "But...wait, what I don't understand..."

"Quick, one vision more!" Fagin said at once, changing the subject, and before Cratchit could finish his thought they faded into a warm, but poor four-room house.

The room was full of children – Bob Cratchit's children – and his good wife was laying a cloth for the dinner table. An old man and a pale, tiny man-child were there, as well, although they stood far apart from the others.

"Bless my soul," the visiting Bob chimed out with joy, "it's my own kith and kin, all together preparing a Christmas feast fit for a king, or at least for those two guests."

"Whatever has got your precious father then?" Mrs. Cratchit said. "And your brother, Tiny Tim! And Martha warn't as late last Christmas by half an hour."

As Bob watched with the Ghost, smiling at the warmth and goodness of his family, a voice ripped through and interrupted his attention.

"Cratchit! What in the blazes are you doing here?!"

At first, Bob was unsure where the sound came from or to which of the family it was addressed. But when it repeated – "Bob Cratchit. You, sir. What are you doing here? This is my vision of things that were!" – he was shocked it was from none other than Mr. Scrooge, the old man he saw across the room and not a guest at all. And the man-child with him was the Ghost of Christmas Past.

"Hallo, Fagin," the man-child Apparition called. "Good to see you, but you have created an awkward situation here. Four's a crowd, you know."

"Here's Martha, mother!" two young Cratchits cried out. "Hurrah."

"Cratchit! I insist you leave!" old Mr. Scrooge angrily scolded the shadow Bob.

"Now, now," the man-child Ghost admonished his elderly charge. "You've been doing so well up to this point."

"Bless my soul, it's all right, for I know how he turns out. This is my guide's fault alone for being here," Bob apologized.

"Oh, you're blaming me now?" Fagin spit out. "Take care, I say. Remember, I can make your life a living hell. Literally."

The two youngest Cratchits yelled out, "There's father coming. "Hide, Martha!"

"Oh, wonderful, now two of him are going to be in the room," Scrooge moaned to the man-child. "Don't try to tell me this is a shadow of what has been."

"They are what they are," said that same small Ghost. "Do not blame me!"

The room was become as like a circus. Children running to hide, Mrs. Cratchit scurrying to ready the house, Scrooge and the Ghost of Christmas Past getting in an argument, Cratchit's other self about to arrive, and his older personage thrust into the room by yet a second Spirit, ever-complaining. "Remove me!" Cratchit exclaimed with force. "Now, Fagin. Haunt me no longer! This very instant!"

Fagin's eyes became steely, harsher than Cratchit had ever seen. "Don't you use that tone and think you can order me around. I have friends. And it's not like you've been a sleigh ride in the park," he sneered. "I'll remove you when I'm ready to remove you. And I ain't ready yet."

Bob turned to the others. "Did you know that Fagin here took my pocket watch? It's true. He claimed that…"

The scene instantly changed. Bob saw he was in his own bedroom of his own house of his own neighborhood of his own city of his own country, England. And best of all, he was alone. Not alone in England, of course, but in his bedroom.

Cratchit was exhausted, and it was so early in the morning, too, as good a reason to be exhausted under any circumstance. His bed never had looked so inviting. He crawled in, pulled the quilt up – all the way over his head, just to be safe – and smiled, knowing that at last he was a man without Spirit. Not in the sense of the emotional kind, but the other. And he was soon fast asleep.

For the nonce.

STAVE THREE

IN WHICH THE MIDDLE OF THE THREE SPIRITS MAKES ITS PRESENCE KNOWN

It was a comforting slumber that Cratchit had, it was. His snoring never so sonorous as it was then, denoting here was a man who had earned his rest. Peaceful, it was too, as Bob lay there dreaming of a white Christmas, just like the one falling outside at that very moment. O holy night, at last this was Noël.

Then his clock gonged one. In fact, all of his clocks gonged one. As they were not equally set, though, they did not each ring at the same time, so it sounded like it was eight o'clock. But then he realized the hour. And thus it was that Bob Cratchit waited.

He thought he might have heard voices, but the sounds were too indistinct. Words such as, "No." Or "I won't do it."

And possibly "You take him – Not me – Ask another – It's Christmastime – I have plans – Don't ask again – No, no – Please go away…" But eventually this ceased, and as far as Cratchit could tell, hearing only the creaking of wood joints, it was all just the wind.

The two o'clock hour came. And went. Maybe they're just rude, he thought. You wouldn't think Spirits would be rude, although that last one was. Clearly they do need pocket watches. Cratchit began to get drowsy again.

The bedroom clock chimed the half hour, and just as Cratchit had decided that it was all a dream, he heard a rattling sound, and in through his closed door a figure passed.

"Humbug!" came a voice, cutting through the darkness.

"Mr. Scrooge?? What are you doing here?!"

As moonlight shined through the window, Scrooge's figure could be made out. "Let us just say the holidays are a difficult time to get volunteers, and leave it at that. I warned you of three Spirits, and three you shall have, so we meet yet again."

"Bless my soul."

"That is what we are trying to do. But much still remains up to you."

"So, you are the second Spirit then, the Ghost of Christmas Present."

"Do I look like the fat and jolly Ghost of Christmas Present? Do I appear to weigh twice what I should?" Scrooge asked with a slight annoyance. "Thank you very much. Thank you very very very much." And with a snort added, "I am Ebeneezer Scrooge, for goodness sake. Think, man."

As Cratchit got out of bed, a beatific smile suddenly crossed his face. Scrooge noted with pleasure the change already in Cratchit, but Bob explained he was just happy because he had found his other slipper.

"But make no mistake, Mr. Scrooge," he said as he humbly walked up to the Ghost, "I learnt much last night. Lead on, Spirit." He put his hand out.

"What's that for?" Scrooge inquired, figuring that Cratchit meant to shake his hand, and so he obliged.

"I thought I had to touch your robe so we could leave here to another vision."

Scrooge laughed a hearty laugh. "Oh, no, we just say that to give confidence. You really think you have to touch a piece of cloth so that you can fly?! Ha ha ha!" Oh, my, when Scrooge laughed, there were few in this good old world who could laugh half so fine. Cratchit found it somewhat condescending, but figured that if a ghost was laughing you were ahead of the game, so it was of no great matter.

The room was transformed into a crowded thoroughfare of the city, the multitudes bustling with the vibrancy of the season.

Making their way to a storefront for the wayward, indigent and miserable, Bob noted the poor creatures making their own way inside for comfort. "Here," said Scrooge, handing a five-pound note to Cratchit. "We each have five pounds to give away as we will. Let's see how we manage our affairs."

Cratchit was determined to show up the old fellow that he knew a thing or two about giving to charity. At last, he saw a near-helpless woman crawling bleary-eyed with hunger towards the door, one arm in a sling, her throat rasped from a tubercular cough, and slapping her body for heat as she had no coat. Aye, there's the one who could use a hand more than most, Cratchit noted astutely, and he dropped his fiver into her pocket.

"You're certain then, this is your choice, she is the beneficiary of your generosity, not any of these," Scrooge pointed to the other lost unfortunates heading inside.

"Most indeed."

Scrooge shook his head and muttered, "Tsk, a waste, man," as he led Cratchit into the hospice. They passed by a teeming mass of the needy being served warm cabbage; and given scarves, mittens, and mattresses to lay upon. In the back was a knobby desk where the patron, a jolly, happy soul with a corncob pipe a and button nose, his two eyes made to look larger than they were by enormous spectacles, was going over his ledgers.

"Now, I will show what to have done with five pounds," Scrooge said and he slapped it on the tabletop. When the patron pushed aside his book, he noticed the note to much surprise, "How did I miss that?," he sputtered, and added it to his cash drawer, updating his accounts.

Cratchit was taken aback, that with so many around them in the most dire of straights, how could the Spirit merely pass along his money for bookkeeping?

Scrooge looked at his former clerk as if he were not former, and Cratchit recalled well that beady expression. "Look about you, man, the gentleman here receives specially low costs from those who know of his charity needs. A shilling goes so farther here than a farthing elsewhere. Think,

Cratchit," Scrooge snipped. "You helped one destitute person for a month, if she lasts that long. I helped a concern sustain itself so that it could assist this entire roomful who will be here for many years to come."

And with that, he strode out the door, with a humbled, understanding Cratchit a step behind.

Everywhere the Apparition took Cratchit, the same occurred. Scrooge would pass money for reasons that, when explained, were as if a window to insight had been opened. Acts of charity turned out to be, in truth, cold commerce, and cold commerce took on a life of charity. A would-be thief discovered a bag of coins and thus the store he had his sights upon was spared, a student discovered the tuition to graduate for which a waiting job required that very diploma, a litigant was given the retainer to hire a new barrister able to settle a many-decades old case of inheritance that released funds allowing factories to re-open, several street ladies of pleasure had the pleasure of finding enough money to quit and start other work that in turn forced those malefactors who had employed them out of their wicked business and into honest ways, as well, which as chance would have it, turned out to be a service that benefited from those re-opened factories which hired them because one of their new aides was that self-same, recent university graduate whose oldest friend's cousin was a man who owned the business.

Cratchit took this all in with wonder and some unease, as well, as like a wave was rushing over him. Scrooge tugged at his sleeve. "Come. Another visit this Christmas."

His companion stopped of a sudden. "I beg you take me home, Spirit. I can go no further like this." Cratchit refused another step. "I thought this night's journey would be short and so remained in my dressing gown. Please, Spirit, return me home so that I may at last dress proper."

"You always try my patience, Cratchit. Yet you are like a tarnished metal that but needs buffing to discover the gold. If a silk cravat helps provide that lustre, so be it."

Before you could say Mary, Queen of Scots, they were back in Cratchit's good old room, and Bob rummaged through his good old wardrobe.

"If you take until Easter," Scrooge impatiently chided. "You don't want to know who would rise to be your escort on that day."

Cratchit stepped into the room, tired still, but attired at last. A warm but stylish dark coat, good for traveling; and highest importance of all, comfortable shoes. "By the by, Mr. Scrooge, I realized that if you added the letter 's' to the word 'present,' it would make you the Ghost of Christmas Presents! What a deeper meaning that gives this all."

Scrooge thoughtfully weighed Cratchit's words. "We are engaged with the most profound mysteries of spirit, fate and the human essence here, and you want to find a deeper meaning?!" he finally snapped. "And I told you – I am not the Ghost of Christmas Present. Come. Enough. We are off."

Before Cratchit could reply, he found himself with the Ghost in a dark alleyway, the snow inhospitably blowing about them. A man was pounding himself to keep warm, and when Bob noticed it was none other than Alfred Jingle, the chap for whom he'd bought dinner that very night – or whatever very night it was, Cratchit was becoming bewildered by all of this traveling – his heart sank, and his hand went to find yet more money to give the fellow.

"Stop it!" Scrooge snapped. "If we were here to help this gentleman, I would sing your praises. But the chorus will have to wait."

A door leading into the alley opened, and a woman stepped out of his favorite tavern, the George and Vulture. Cratchit recognized his thoughtful barmaid, Nancy.

"Wondering when you would get here. Like to freeze my toes off. Bitterly cold, very," Jingle chattered through his teeth.

"Well duckie, I can't leave work 'ere before my shift is finished now, can I?"

"Small talk over. Time to account."

The woman made a pile of the money Cratchit had given her as an excessive gratuity, and her cohort combined it with the generous bank notes Bob had handed him when thinking the man impoverished.

"This was a game of swindle they played on me!" Cratchit sputtered. "He is not poor, and she knew him from the first."

Scrooge nodded with a world-weary assurance. "And they fobbed you into buying him a great feast on top of it. Quite a nice Christmas present. Or should I say," he added with a sardonic look, "ghost of Christmas present."

Although Cratchit felt the fool, what he discovered there in the blizzard was that the truth really does set you free, albeit at a cost. So much charity had been wasted that should have gone to others.

"I should like to follow the scoundrel to find where he lives," Bob stated. "And I know where the lady works."

The Ghost placed a restraining arm on Cratchit's shoulder. "It is interesting you should mention work. There is something you needs see."

The scene changed, and they were in the offices of Scrooge & Marley. The earlier snow of the evening had become ever more intense, pounding the streets as the temperature dropped bitterly. The weather outside was frightful, but inside, Cratchit could see, it was so delightful with the calming quiet. To think that such a lovely firm as this, that had done so much good, was in so much financial trouble.

The silence was broken by a noise in the back. "Could that not be Mr. Twist working so very late? On Christmas Eve?" Cratchit noted quizzically.

"That would be a fine assumption," the Ghost acknowledged. "But wrong."

"Bless my soul, it's Mr. Heep," and Heep it was, intently going over the firm's year end books with swift industry, his labour in the pitch dark lit by only a lone candle.

"Carry the seven, move the nine, lose the debit, lose the debit, wherever shall it go?" the wiry fellow gnarled to himself.

Cratchit allowed to Mr. Scrooge as how he was astonished to see his head clerk at work on so holiday a Christmas Eve, in the wee hours, no less, yet he couldn't help feel gratified. Having the accounts squared by the first of January was the very planning the Spirits have been trying to impress upon him! Perhaps a raise was due Mr. Heep.

Scrooge refrained from shaking Cratchit senseless. "Are you mad, man?! He's not doing you a favor, the thief is stealing you blind! The blackguard is shifting money to himself. He is taking what little last crumbs remain and making his own biscuits from them. He's hiding false accounting books! Just look, man!"

Though never was Bob known for losing his humour, recent events had impacted several changes upon the good gentleman, and one of these was having his choler raised by what larceny he saw before him with his own eyes.

"I can't believe it!" he yawled. "Though I mean, yes, I can believe it because there it is, of course, but I mean I cannot believe the man would do such a thing."

"A trusting nature is good for the soul, but bad for the bottom line," the Ghost stated, adding with a shrug, "When you live in eternity, you have a good deal of time to think up proverbs."

Cratchit wasn't thinking about eternity at the moment, except as a place to send Heep. He was comforted by remembering that time heals all wounds, though observed that he'd like to wound this heel.

It was the second deception that Cratchit had discovered yet that night. In his ire, it came to him that Heep himself should be visited by three ghosts, "but really bad ones." Scrooge was not swayed by temporal impatience. He was here with a greater purpose.

"I have but two visions more to show you," the Ghost told him. "Maybe three, we'll see."

The scene transformed, and the travelers were in the elegant salon of an even more elegant home.

A well-dressed, gray-haired, respectable old gentleman was patting his stomach as his other hand held a snifter of warm brandy. "The finest Christmas dinner since last year, I dare say, and that was the finest Christmas dinner that ever was ." The half dozen others heartily agreed, even though most hadn't been at the previous Christmas dinner. But they were good people of decent hearts every last one of them, and they knew that if Mr. Brownlow[15] spoke it, it must be so.

Amid this gracious splendor, to Cratchit's immense

---

[15] Mr. Brownlow.

Editor's note: When Dickens wrote Oliver Twist, he had painted himself into a corner with the plot, unable to figure out how to give Oliver's story – that had gone deep into the underbelly of London's dark, sordid, criminal society – a happy, cheery ending. Stuck, he came up with the first of his wild coincidences that latter populated several of his novels, or "just happens to happen" that Dickens called them, and mastered. He had young Oliver, who just happens to be on his very first pickpocketing mission ever, and just happens to do so terribly that he actually gets caught and just happens to have chosen as his very first victim a man who just happens to be his grandfather, who just happens to be wealthy and benevolent, and ends up taking Oliver under his wing for a life of leisure and ease. This turned out too much for his publisher who begged Dickens tone it down, which Dickens reluctantly acquiesced to, though the only change he ultimately did was make the old man, Mr. Brownlow, a friend of the family, not Oliver's grandfather. "Oh, my, that's so much better and so less coincidental," the publisher wrote sarcastically in his diary.

surprise in walked none other than his apprentice, Mr. Twist. They young man was impeccably dressed and showed the ease of noblesse even amongst such a fine crowd. Bob watched in open-jawed wonder.

"The young man is heir to all this," the Ghost informed him. "Brownlow had been his guardian as an orphan boy."

If you had told Cratchit he himself had been crowned King of all England, he would not have been more stunned. That is an exaggeration, but the general idea remains. "I thought young Mr. Twist was poor as the day is long."

"Poor of heart, seeing the many bad ways your business is being run," Scrooge explained, "very rich elsewhere. It pains him knowing the firm he admires is in such dire straits. For what other reason do you think he spends so much time working so hard for so little? It has no future. Yet he wishes to give it one."

Cratchit had no answer. He always just figured his apprentice desperately needed work experience, or perhaps had nowhere else to go. Yet Bob now felt a pride swell in his breast that such a grand person would willingly expend himself on his behalf.

"Bless my soul, there's more to me than meets the eye," he marveled.

Mr. Twist was seated with Brownlow, deep in private conversation, bringing his chair closer that the two might speak in earnest.

"I wish I could say the firm will succeed, it does much good, and I know well from my workhouse days and my dark days after, when need caused me to fall in with pickpockets, how profoundly such deeds are needed. But I fear it cannot last long, which is why I've come to you."

He explained his plan, that once Scrooge & Marley's went bankrupt, which alas he anticipated soon, to act quickly to retain its physical assets and accounts, and refinance the company to run efficiently by setting up separate commercial and charity divisions kept apart for legal protection, asking if Brownlow would consider being an investor.

"Now, why didn't I think of any of that?" Cratchit asked in wonderment.

"Perhaps because you don't know what you are doing," Scrooge answered. "Though that's only a guess, you understand."

Brownlow listened carefully, and the amount he proffered was generous, but only a start of what Twist felt was required.

"A wery fine plan it is," said a lively guest, leaning forward. "I 'opes you don't mind my listening, but when I sees two such weritable gentlemen in so serious a confabulation, I can't help but admire. And as I know more than a few people, as the bishop said to his congregation, I may have the answer to your problems."

The two were more than interested in listening to their friend. "If any man has a quick way around an obstacle, Sam Weller,[16] it's you," Brownlow noted.

---

[16] Sam Weller.

Editor's note: Sam Weller was Mr. Pickwick's exuberant, fast-talking, Cockney valet, who turned out to be a wildly

"As it so 'appens, I know another young gent what's got as fine a connection to big money as 'e does kindness. I believe that Oliver and Mr. Nickleby will become best of acquaintances, I do. And all I asks is just 'earty thanks – and a five percent finder's fee," Weller said with a wink and a laugh, though he meant it.

Cratchit was much taken with all this fascinating world of business conversation. "Assets and debits," he called to Scrooge. "Who would have thought it!"

Scrooge could only look skyward and speak to an unseen presence. "Now you see why I said I needed to come here?!"

Cratchit pulled a stool up close, and sat enraptured. He wrote down all he heard, not wanting to miss a detail, making a list and checking it twice. But Scrooge said it was time to move on.

"Wait, Spirit, can we not just stay. This is too good to miss. Perhaps you could go on without me, and then return and report back what you saw! That way, we...

As Cratchit spoke, the scene transformed.

It was suddenly bright out, as Cratchit and Scrooge were in

(*cont'd*) popular character with readers. Dickens, however, hadn't introduced Sam until late in the novel of The Pickwick Papers. Feeling that this was a wasted opportunity for so successful a character, who could perhaps be spun-off into his own, full book, the author brought Sam Weller back into this story as a first step towards accomplishing that. Figuring, too, that Weller could help make this story successful.

London Town, with shouts of "Happy Christmas to you and yours" sounding about them everywhere.

"You never let me finish what I'm saying, do you?" Bob asked the Ghost.

"Were it in my power, I would rarely let you start."

They were outside a building crowded with men waiting to enter, while others left at a fevered pace. The two visitors bypassed the line, "One of the advantages of being a vision," the Apparition noted.

The frenetic activity surprised Bob, it being Christmas. Perhaps it was a holiday charity center. At the center of the hurricane was a fellow frenetically giving orders who Cratchit was most astonished and equally happy to find.

"Jack Dawkins! My young, struggling competitor. Bless my soul, back on his feet." Yet he was confused. "It was only last night I saw him in poverty, begging."

"Does he look like he's in poverty?" noted Scrooge in his sarcastic manner so endearing to those not on the receiving end. "Look at the company here. It has accounts twenty times yours and work so overflowing it must open on Christmas. The fellow wasn't begging others! Think, man! He was collecting debts."

People bustled everywhere, giving money, taking money. The only near-spot of quiet was an old lady in the corner, sewing a blanket. Where the grace of age should have given her dignity, a shriveled hand and menacing glare were all she showed.

"Bless my soul and her heart, the dear one so cold she needs have extra warmth and stitches her own mantle. Will no one help this poor soul? Will the pursuit of money blind all here to give aid? This room is Ignorance, and this woman is Want."

"She owns the establishment," Scrooge corrected. "And she knows to protect it, so watch your step, even if you are just a vision. If anyone can wake the dead, it is she."

And running it all, young Mr. Dawkins was a small package of persistent vitality with quick eyes darting everywhere. Jotting figures on a paper, conversing with clerks, exchanging funds in all manner of directions.

"He certainly appears to be doing well here."

"Oh, does he now?" Scrooge commented with a pose of mock surprise.

Cratchit watched in wonderment as Dawkins went to consult with the old woman. Yes, this is what he himself should be doing. "However does he manage so extensive a business with so many great costs, and still have any revenue left over to give?!"

"To start with," the Ghost answered, "he cheats. Nothing illegal, mind you," and here Scrooge paused to consider his words, "that can be seen. In business there is much creativity with the law that even our finest stage talents would applaud for its art."

It was simple. Show higher costs on paper, gain political favors by gift, move income into self-run charities that pay no taxes, re-define investments and losses.

"You have long since justified my wisdom of hiring you after your release from prison in Australia," the old lady spit out with a French accent to her young office director. "You will keep our figures close to the vest, I trust."

Dawkins placed the incriminating papers close to his vest in theory and in fact, and then further beneath his coat which he tightly buttoned. "It is a mutual trust, Madame Defarge[17], that I trust will grow to even greater mutual benefit."

She returned to her blanket, not a blanket for warmth, as Cratchit had supposed, but he saw that she was instead stitching in the names of investors who had not paid what they had promised.

---

[17] Madame Defarge.

Editor's note: As a young man, Dickens was fascinated with hidden words and codes, finding them in all manner of instances, both real and imagined. He saw ciphers in the law books he read when a court reporter and in government documents that occasionally came into his possession, but also in chalk drawings he'd come across on the sidewalk. He also had a favorite sweater that had been made for him by an aunt who had passed away before Dickens had received it. For the rest of his life he was sure that his aunt had woven a secret message to him from beyond the grave that would reveal the secrets of the universe. Such was the inspiration of Madame Defarge. So taken was he, too, by the possibility that something secret had been written in his very own words for this character, that he brought her back in A Tale of Two Cities as a leader of the French revolution who wove the names of her enemies into fabrics, since Dickens hoped that he might finally decode what he himself meant.

Cratchit marveled at what Defarge and Dawkins had done. Certainly their actions were deceitful, and not at all defensible except with very good attorneys, yet imagine he said what good could be done if one worked on the same idea but legally, to collect much money so that you could actually give more! He strode outside, anxious to see the bright world of glorious possibilities around him.

As he met the sunlight, it was like wisdom bursting within his head. He spun to Scrooge. "All their revenue is like an endowment that could provide charity, loans and funds for investment for so many years to come!"

"Can your firm say the same?" the Ghost inquired.

As Cratchit began to speak, he suddenly found himself outside Scrooge & Marley, which provided the answer: there were no lines of those in need out front, no bustling of helpful activity inside, the door locked and the paint faded and peeling upon the walls.

He took his keys out to unlock the door. "Spirit, I have seen so much over who-knows how many days. And I know now what lies befo…" As he entered the office, the room transformed itself. "Oh, come now! At least give me a chance once to…"

He and Mr. Scrooge now stood in a large dining room. Except for one table the room was empty, as was the rest of the inn, for that is where it was. That solitary table however was set for a feast, highlighted by a crisp roasted goose and steaming plate of Christmas haggis. Seated at the head of this table (though not precisely the head as it was round) was a good-natured matron whose good nature was clearly being tested.

"My dear missus!" Cratchit cried, for it was she. "Bless my soul, it's good to see her on such a holiday that I thought to have spent apart. Happy times, indeed."

Happy times for the absent father perhaps, but for the rest, not so much. The two eldest, Peter and Belinda, sat almost unmoving except for when they looked at each other and rolled their eyes, heaving a sigh. The two little ones, neither quite yet eighteen, were not so unmoving, shifting in their seats as if the chairs were afire. The only sound heard was coughing and rampant sniffling, the residual of spending December in Scotland.

"Wherever could your brother Tall Tim be?" Mrs. Cratchit at last wondered aloud, checking the doorway yet again, and yet again it was empty.

"He knows when dinner was supposed to be, mother," Peter snapped. "Can't we just start. The goose is getting cold. And the haggis, well, no one really cares."

"We'll wait a little longer," their mother replied and then sneezed. "This is Christmas, it is, and if Christmas teaches us anything, it is patience."

The two older children looked at each other askance. "No, it doesn't," Peter said. "That has nothing to do with the message of Christmas." His sister stared at her plate and made a rude face it in, as the boy continued, sneezing first. "This is so terribly unfair, we shouldn't have to hear our stomachs grumble just because Tim is late. Again."

The two youngest decided that if they had to wait further, they could do so by not waiting, at the table at least, and began chasing each other 'round the room, neither quite certain after a while which one was chasing the other, crashing into chairs and tumbling.

"I don't even want to be here," Belinda finally spoke up. "And neither does Peter." He shot her a look, and she glared back. "Well, you don't, you told me so," and spun back to her mother. "I had the chance to be with my beau, and Peter was invited join his young lady's family in Italy. But instead we're in Scotland where no one else comes, you may have noticed, hardly a family together, you may have noticed, and we've all caught colds. I wish I were dead." She sneezed and coughed. "And soon, I may be."

"It's Christmas, daughter," Mrs. Cratchit answered, "be kind for the little ones."

"The little ones are no longer so little, you may have noticed, and no longer need protection," snapped the girl, "except perhaps to shield their heads against running into another wall. The only reason they're not bored is because they have not the wits to be."

Scrooge turned to Cratchit. "I never mentioned to you how sorry I am that I wasn't able to join your family for the holidays more often."

"I cherish them all dearly," he responded proudly. "And sometimes more dearly from afar."

At that moment, in walked Tall Tim, a strapping lad with a bold step and equally bold call. "Here's Tim, all! Here's Tim at last. Home he is, or home away from home."

"Hurrah, Tim! Hurrah," the two youngest cried out. "It's Tim, mother. Hurrah."

"Oh, hurrah," the eldest brother muttered. "Now, may we eat, mother?" he asked, but first she inquired of Tim what caused his delay.

Tim explained he had gone to the local church and stood outside as parishioners arrived, reminding them upon this day who made lame beggars walk and blind men see.

"Jesus," Peter said, his teeth clenched.

"Indeed, so I told them," Tim noted. "But after a time, they got the constable, who brought me to the stationhouse on a charge of vagrancy. I reminded him of the day, and seeing I brought no danger, he let me be to my family feast. And at last, I've come."

"Last. Yes, that's the word I was searching for," Peter called out.

"The family is together," Mrs. Cratchit announced, "save your father and…" she hesitated, as she looked to her side, "…and one who is missed very much. We do so miss Martha." The bickering and some of the coughing stopped, as all became silent.

"Spirit," said Cratchit with deep emotion, "tell me what happened."

"I see a vacant seat," replied the Ghost, "next to where she would have otherwise sat beside to her mother."

"Oh, no, Spirit, tell me that the shadows may change."

"Martha has a family of her own now, and last evening felt it would not be wise to keep small children in such a cold and damp clime. Her argument with her mother was most harsh. If these shadows remain unaltered, your child may not return."

"No, Spirit, say our family will be spared and will all be as one next Christmas!"

"If these shadows remain unaltered, no other Spectre will find her with you at another Yuletide trip. Cratchit hung his head in sadness.

"Now, can we eat?" Peter pleaded. "While I still have strength to lift my fork?"

"I give you the founder of the feast, your father," Mrs. Cratchit sang out.

Peter dove for the food, but Tall Tim beat him to it. "And the last shall be first," Peter grumbled, finally loading his plate, as did all the rest. Belinda though just stabbed at a few peas with her fork, tapping away with the tines aimlessly.

"Founder of the feast, indeed," she finally said. "If I found him here, that would be another matter. But he's not here, if you may have noticed."

"Your dear father," Mrs. Cratchit started, "is with us in spirit."

"If she only knew!" Scrooge laughed.

"He is here amongst us in your very being and we together at this inn, just as the Child who we celebrate was. Your father has obligations to help the destitute and spread the goodness of the season, just as we should expect the Father of us all to do this day."

"My, she is very good at that," the Ghost noted. "Very quick with the retort."

"That's my dear one," Cratchit agreed. "You don't get past her without having an armada overstocked with ammunition."

"If we sold Tall Tim, how many destitute people do you

think we could feed for a year?" Peter inquired.

The two little ones started giggling, which led to them coughing. As sympathy lends comfort in numbers, Belinda started in to cough, as well, and then mightily sneeze. Peter did sneeze, likewise, and his youngest siblings joined him. And in time the whole of them were sneezing one on top of the other.

Their brother Tall Tim, having spent much of his holiday time away upon the highlands, had not yet caught the cold of his family. "God bless you, everyone," he called. "To your health of the season. And I can only remind you all upon this day of your indisposition who it was that made lame beggars walk and blind…"

Suddenly, a bun came flying across the table and hit him square in the middle of the face. "And who was it," Peter laughed, "that made bloody noses clot?"

Immediately upon receipt, Tall Tim took up a potato and flung it back at his older brother, with a force most impressive, hitting him in the chest.

"Children, children!" Mrs. Cratchit cried out, "Not on such a day. Think of the gifts of food the Wise Men brought on this very eve, and be wise your …"

"Oh, mother, do not make this any more than it is," her daughter shouted back. "It is two brothers getting into a tiff, not a representation of the Last Supper."

At once, mother and daughter were amid arguing, voices raised, as food went soaring past. The youngest Cratchits leaped from their seats and began circling the table, tackling one another.

"Perhaps," Father Cratchit off-handedly suggested, as he ducked a piece of cake, "we could visit yet another Christmas gathering?"

"No. No, I think we will stay here for a spell," Scrooge taunted him. "Let you experience a Christmas feast with the family. Charity begins at home, does it not? "

"Please, Spirit, I recognize the joy of being with one's family," Cratchit entreated, "but one must know his fellow men everywhere to understand mankind. We do a disservice to such knowledge by remaining here."

"All you needs do," Scrooge explained with a sly chuckle, "is open the door."

Without appearing too anxious, Cratchit strode towards the knob, quickening his pace as he neared the blessèd exit. And with one last look behind, he stepped through.

Lo the difference! Away from the babel of shouts, away from cold walls and colder intents, away from the shouting of day merely because another called night.

Instead, Cratchit stood upon a low hillock, fresh-fallen snow bedded atop the ground, that was like Eden to him. Below was a glow from the streetlights of London.

"Spirit, take me home now," replied a relieved Cratchit, as the ever-familiar bells of Big Ben struck eleven. "I wish to be in my bed."

"You and everyone. But soon another Ghost will lead you on your journey. My time upon this land grows short. Thank goodness."

"I know I have much yet to learn, Spirit – "

The bells chimed three-quarters after eleven, as Cratchit spoke.

" – for I have seen so much already, and...." He stopped a moment, as something seemed odd. "That was an exceptionally fast forty-five minutes, was it not?"

"Then, you'd best talk quickly if you have any last words to me" Scrooge noted.

Cratchit was flustered. He spoke fast as he could, "I want you to know that w..."

The bells chimed twelve. "That can't have been fifteen minutes!" Bob shouted. Annoyed, he spun to see if the hour truly was of midnight. Turning back, however, he found that Scrooge had given up the ghost. Cratchit was alone.

But not so alone as he thought. For with dread, Cratchit sensed another presence, Of course, at this point, his state was such that the mere wisp of a snowflake would have made him sense something was amiss, but then this was no wisp. Cratchit saw before him the robed and hooded figure of a Phantom, standing against the blackness of the sky.

"Halloo," Cratchit chirped hopefully. "How d'ye do?"

The Phantom said not a word.

Stave Four

THE THIRD AND THEREFORE FINAL OF THE THREE SPIRITS, OR SO BOB CRATCHIT HOPES, UNLESS THINGS DON'T GO WELL IN WHICH CASE HE'S PRAYING FOR A FOURTH TO WORK THINGS OUT

There upon the hill, the world seemed suddenly very dark to Cratchit. Being just past midnight aided this impression no doubt, but so too did the Phantom before him, a thick black robe covering its heavy frame, if frame it was, nothing so much as visible.

"Spirit, tell me, are you the Ghost whose presence was foretold me? For if not, given some of the problems I have seen tonight, it is not beyond the realm of possibilities that you mean to haunt someone else instead and may be lost. Besides which, now that I think of it, it's midnight, and I was told my Ghost would be here at one."

The Apparition held up a hand not like a hand at all, which stopped Cratchit from speaking. It moved in a haphazard way as Spirits are wont to do that brought itself nearer to Bob, who would have moved farther away if he could, which in fact he could but didn't, frozen where he stood and not by the cold.

"Ghost of Christmas Yet to Come, I fear you the most of all," he shook. "It is not personal, I'm sure you're a fine fellow, but when three ghosts come to teach one a lesson, one must assume something dire has a strong chance of happening, and that leaves you." The silence Cratchit heard was more deafening than a thunderclap. "Can you not speak?"

Once more, the Spirit put up its hand that held a turkey drumstick, which turned out to be what Cratchit had thought its unearthly fingers, and finished chewing. "So sorry there, caught me in the midst of dinner when they asked me to come here they did, quite the rush it was, I only had time to throw on this old cloak I did, and lost all track of time and got here an hour early, as I live and breathe, which I suppose I don't, ha ha ha! ...A moment, if you please."

As the Spectre chuckled on to himself, he wiped his hands in the folds of his tattered robe. His hood fell back, revealing a head looking like a large melon, or perhaps like a large head. His face was full, as was the rest of his stout body beneath it.

"Ghost of the Future!," Bob called out, "I hope to be a

better businessman than I was. As I know your reason for being here is good," (though Cratchit knew that not, but what he did know was that it never hurt to get on the good side of a Wraith), "lead on."

"I do believe you have me confused with another," the figure before him noted, "I'm hardly the Ghost of Any Christmas, especially thems what's Yet to Come, though I do know the fellow, a good chap, a fine chap, a solid chap, but a bit sullen at times, I must say. Refused to come here he did for some reason or other, but I weren't told. I do know they tried to get this nice Jewish gent, but oh my, he wanted no part of it. Something to do with having a sick relative, Aunt Semitism, I believe her name were, but no matter and no mind to me. I was eating dinner with my dear wife Mrs. McCawber, a lovely woman if ever there was, you must meet her, though not until you've died, of course, and let's hope that's a long time from now. What was I telling you? Oh, yes, someone asked me as to get over here, 'Get down there, McCawber[18],' they says to

---

[18] Mr. McCawber.

From Dickens' notes. "Just finished writing the character of the Ghost of Christmas Yet to Come, Mr. McCawber. Gave the section to my sister Fanny, who says the character reads exactly like our father. Oh, my, dear Fanny, no. It is simply not so. Try as I might, I don't see it at all. Absolutely Not At All. I have not the slightest idea what in the world she is talking about. I love my dear sister as much as I love my cherished and most-revered father, but she is completely wrong. And I should know my own work. I fear she is idealizing that great, wonderful, dear, glorious man.

me, 'we need somebody, anybody,' and if a man can't help a fellow friend, who can you help?, and it sounded rather jolly, it did. So, here I am, and it's a pleasure to make your acquaintance."

Not certain how to take this greeting, Bob was sure that a pleasant word trumped hellfire at any time. And so he cautiously allowed it was nice to meet the Spirit, as well.

"But for what you will show me tonight of my future, are these things that will be or things that may be?" he asked, filled with dread. "Or they could be, but aren't fully certain? Or they all should happen, unless something else occurs to change them first?"

McCawber peered at his charge with the good nature that was his. "Well, that's a muckle of fish," he gurgled. "The future is the future. How am I supposed to know what will happen? It hain't happened yet! I should think that was fairly obvious. Will what I am to show you happen?" he crunched

---

(*cont'd*) McCawber is just a fun, little character. I had a such good, grand, oh-so happy time with. I miss him already in the story and would do most anything to have him still at my fingertips. It's hard not to admire his overwhelming charm and virtue." When Dickens wrote David Copperfield, an admittedly semi-autobiographical work, he included Mr. McCawber yet again, in a tour-de-force characterization of a wonderfully good-hearted man always out of money and often in debtors prison, a portrayal which all scholars readily acknowledge is blatantly based almost exactly to a "t" on Dickens's father.

his eyes deep in thought, so as to give the question its full due. "It certainly could. Who knows?! But let's say we find out!"

As the two headed down towards the city, Cratchit was happy that the future he was about to see was not definite. On the other hand, all these things might happen, the Spirit wasn't clear on that point, or on most any point, for that matter. Cratchit wondered too why they were walking to their destination, rather than just appearing there.

But whatever the future held, Cratchit looked at it with deep foreboding.

Making their way, McCawber explained his theory of how best to keep dry during a rainstorm, a long tale that concluded with the suggestion to "stay indoors," and then moved into a deliberation on home furnishings, the state of forests within England, and a meandering history of the Celts, several dates of which were incorrect. As they turned a corner, it had become noontime (for that was how long this had taken). Ahead, Bob was relieved to see a couple of gentlemen he recognized, fellow souls of his profession.

"On my word, it's sad what happened to him, he was a good man," the first noted.

"All men have goodness," his friend replied, "it's what you do with it that matters. And he foolishly threw it all away."

"Well, I for one feel sorry for him."

"Little thought he gave to those poor creatures whose lives will be hurt by his ineptitude, now that his firm is shut down."

Cratchit listened with fascination. The unfortunate fellow

whose life had been ruined by incompetence at business and thoughtless extravagance in charity. "Who are these men speaking of, Spirit?"

McCawber looked at him with an expression of stupefaction. "Certainly, you're not serious?" When Cratchit assured him that he was, the Ghost cried out, "You! You, man, they are talking about you! That's you."

"Bless my soul," a concerned Cratchit averred at this turn of future events. "I've done rather poorly."

The Ghost provided a hand on Bob's shoulder. "Well, don't I know from being poorly? As I said to my dear Mrs. McCawber only yesterday, I says to her it's a poor man what's doing poorly, but then don't that shining woman answer back, 'McCawber, just give a fellow a stick in his hand, a song in his heart and a big sack of gold and see if he ain't still poor," oh, what a fine wife, she is, and there's no mistaking. What was I saying?" Cratchit offered that it was about his doing poorly. "Ah, yes, but the point here is that it's not you who's done most poorly, but them."

"Who is them?"

The Spirit pointed with an outstretched arm. And Cratchit saw that the district was now full of thousands lining the street, pushing each other, the avenue overwhelmed. The crush of humanity was almost too much for Cratchit to bear.

"All these poor souls are destitute for my failure?" he cried out. "Oh, woe is me!"

"What, these folks?" McCawber asked. "No, no, they came to see the Christmas Day parade. I was referring to them," and again he pointed, observing six people on a float highlighted by a large sign, "People Left Homeless Because of Bob Cratchit."

"That's all?" Cratchit inquired. "Half a dozen?" He began to feel a bit better.

"Oh, don't be silly. Only six could fit in the wagon. There's a list as long as my arm," McCawber explained, "They'd have gotten a bigger lorry, but couldn't afford it."

The concern that had just so recently left Cratchit made a sudden return visit. "I know them all, I assisted them all. Has it come to this?"

"One story as lamentable as the next. Take that sorry gent," McCawber noted.

Cratchit recognized the fellow in question, for whom he had long made charitable contributions anonymously. "And now he's on the street," he choked.

"That hain't the half of it. When he didn't pay rent, the landlord defaulted to his loan company and a project it was financing fell through. That caused the contractors to go under, which brought about a run on several banks, and the economic crisis forced out the government. A weakened England led to civil uprising in Europe, which grew to war.

Cratchit was aghast, which is putting it mildly. "Tell me this isn't true!"

"Of course it hain't true!" McCawber shouted. "But you thought it could be, you thought the sorrow of one single person could be the sorrow of all Man. And so it is.

If Cratchit wasn't still shaking so much, he would have attempted to throttle the Spirit before him, though he soon realized that McCawber had a point.

"Besides," the Ghost continued, "just because the world's not falling apart don't mean their lives hain't. Do you recognize anyone you know?"

They were now outside a pub in a quiet neighborhood. A reedy thin gentleman in a baggy red vest wore an oversized waistcoat that draped over him and trod slowly along the snow. Cratchit racked his memory for a connection, but could find none.

Just then, another man walked by and tipped his hat to the first, "Afternoon to you, Pickwick. Happy Christmas and the season" and strolled away.

Cratchit was shocked near beyond words, "That's Mr. Pickwick?!" he cried. "He's so thin. The last I saw him, he was so..." he looked at McCawber and at that Ghost's own very large girth, and hesitated out of politeness."

"So fat. Not to worry, Mr. Cratchit. We of the fraternity know well our shape. But alas and alack and aday, Mr. Pickwick has fallen on hard times, and your benefices have long run out. Lose pounds in the wallet, and you lose pounds everywhere else."

Cratchit watched the now-gaunt Pickwick amble off. "I must say though, he does look healthier. All that weight could not have been good for him to carry."

When they continued through town, a majestic edifice towered before him, and Cratchit's introspection was lifted. There is nothing like a soaring house of faith to make one's very own faith soar. Many floors high this temple was, with spires aplenty, rose windows, ornate columns, all designed to impose and impress, and they did that and more. Flocks of people lined up deep to get inside.

"It does my heart good," Bob avowed, "to see a cathedral so grand and even more desired. I am joyful that in the future yet to come, what was good of faith is ever still."

"Correct me if I'm mistaken," the Ghost said, "but you appear to be suggesting that this is a church. This is the home office for the firm of Madame Defarge and Jack Dawkins. They have counting-houses across the country, all of which report here."

Cratchit was startled beyond measure, a condition he was beginning to find familiar. The firm of D & D had become a mighty force. With Scrooge & Marley gone and other competition driven to failure, the company could set whatever standards it wanted, and what it wanted was everything. Reliance upon it was king.

"Business may be a wondrous thing," the Spirit noted, "but business without competition is nobody's business. This hain't business you see afore you. This is tyranny, tyranny, says I!, and it lives, says I, because you abandoned the first principle of business, and that is to have principal, which you don't have, and without it, it don't matter how many principles you do have. Money, sir, you need money, says McCawber. For with none, you ran your firm into the ground, and what grew from your buried principles is tyranny, and that hain't business. Says McCawber!"

Cratchit wanted only to get away from that dreadful place, which cast a deep shadow. As he and McCawber turned a corner, Cratchit discovered that they were outside his old office of Scrooge & Marley, which he almost missed since the paint was peeled off, windows boarded up, and the door long-since bolted by order of the law.

Standing under the sulfurous glow of a street lamp, a young girl no more than fourteen sadly stared between the planks into the bolted-up company, a tear streaking down her cheek, her little fingers tightly grasping a cherished toy.

"What child is this at such a late hour?" Cratchit inquired, "and with no reason, as the firm is clearly out of business?"

"She comes each night with only the hope of a miracle to find the place open. Once, she was sustained by charity from here, but now with Scrooge & Marley's closed, all she has left are her memories, the early stages of influenza and a lump of coal."

At that moment, who should step from the shadows but none other than young Mr. Twist! He appeared ragged, as well, and gaunt, a thoughtful but lost look in his eyes.

"Before you asks and also says 'Bless my soul,'" McCawber interrupted Cratchit who was indeed about to do both, "poor Mr. Twist met with hard times when Scrooge & Marley's closed, he did. His plans destroyed, he was refused employ by others for the taint of working at so discredited a firm, and don't I know about that, and my dear Mrs. McCawber will tell you as I do, and a lie couldn't live in that good lady's mouth. What was I saying? Anywhatever, he became evermore bitter and began arguing harshly with his benefactor, who eventually disinherited him and threw him out to the streets."

The young man was still drawn to his old office, where great hopes once ruled, and there he noticed the young child in great want. He kindly offered his name and a handshake, and she softly returned that her name was Nell.

"My, you are a small one," he smiled warmly, the only

warmth the girl had had around her for months. "I shall call you <u>Little Nell</u>[19]."

"I would rather you didn't, sir. It's a bit patronising. Just Nell will be fine."

"Come, this is no place for man, beast or Nell child to be

---

[19] Little Nell.

From the publisher's notes: "Dear Mr. Dickens, I am not quite sure what you are doing. It is one thing to write a character named Tiny Tim, and then another named Little Dorritt, but now to have one named Little Nell? I understand not your thinking, unless it is to create a series of "Little People" books for children. Please desist from doing this. I almost cringe turning the page, in expectation of seeing a new character named Little Tiny Little. I might suggest you write a book with a world made up of Lilliputians, except that Jonathan Swift already did that with his Gulliver's Travels, and much better." To spite Bunderston, with whom his relationship was deteriorating, Dickens not only made Little Nell the central character in his later novel, <u>The Old Curiosity Shop</u>, but intentionally portrayed her as one of the most utterly virtuous, ever-sweet, pure, almost unbelievably noble, saccharine and beyond imaginably kind-hearted characters, the soulful epitome of goodness – who is hounded by an evil, venal, tortuous, twisted hunchback, no doubt a satiric jab at Joseph Bunderston, a character so cruel that Dickens had him drive Little Nell to one of the most famous, tragic, and over-the-top, maudlin deaths in all of literature. And as an added swipe at his publisher, Dickens later created yet another of his "tiny" characters, Little Em'ly, in <u>David Copperfield</u>.

on a cold Christmas night. There's cheer up ahead, I see," and he directed the shivering girl to follow him past where holiday revelers had gathered. The two wayfarers had trouble getting through the crowd, whence Twist had to push others to clear a path for her. Beyond the throng, Oliver handed the child a thick, leather billfold, removing half the notes for himself. "There," he said. "Just for being yourself and hungry and deserving."

Cratchit didn't know what to make of this. "Where did he come by the money, Spirit, for he seems as poor as she?"

The little girl's little eyes bulged until they were no longer little. "Whereforever did you come by this, for you seem as poor as I?"

Oliver rubbed his fingertips together. "It's an old trick I learned once, when I was younger than even you. You see, some gents don't need all their money, and it's up to me to teach them and do a little light lifting." He let her stare at her new-gotten money and dream what she could do with it. "And there's more pockets to pick where that came from. Would you like to learn the trick?"

"Oh, please, sir, yes."

Cratchit had to lean up against McCawber. To see his admired apprentice come down to this, and then bring another so young into larceny was almost too much to bear.

"It's worse, sir," McCawber added. "This hain't the first waif he's approached, but has a whole gang of young 'uns, destitute all. And these thieve throughout the city, all because of one reason. A firm going out of business, and that firm, sir, is yours! That firm I speak of is Scrooge & Marley's."

95

Cratchit was beside himself, or more accurately still beside the Ghost on whom he was leaning for support. "Take me away from this sight, McCawber. Take me so tha…"

Suddenly, the cold street vanished, and Bob was instead –

"What is wrong with all of you?!" he sputtered. "Can't any ghost ever let someone finish a sentence?"

But before McCawber could answer, Cratchit saw he was in the manor hall of an exquisite mansion, and there, his very own family! A Christmas feast like ever there was one on the most sumptuous table if ever there was one, and all dressed in the most elegant fineries if ever there were many.

"Bless my soul, they look so well!" Cratchit exuded. He was overjoyed to see that all had turned out so well. And if his happiness could handle more, which it always could, who was coming down the staircase to make it a happy family once again but his previously-absent daughter, Martha.

"Hurrah, it's Martha!" he cried. "Hurrah!"

And when the two youngest, now nearing their twenties, therefore less young than before, saw their sister, they shouted, as well, "Hurrah, Martha! Hurrah, hurrah!" And they ran to hug her and then raced off, tripping over a chair and crashing into the wall.

And there was his dear wife waltz in, oh my, dressed in a gown fit for the queen, if she wasn't royalty already wearing her tiara and jewels. "Over here, Rose," she directed the servant to clean a smudge on a walnut chest, then another spot to wipe upon a window pane. "A merrier Christmas there ever was for us all!"

"Now, there is a good wife," Cratchit noted to

McCawber, who allowed as she may be, but when it came to good wives, none was finer than his dear Mrs. McCawber, thank you very much. The two argued on the merits of their wives' respective goodness and almost came to blows over it, but for the wonderful emotions they felt.

"As it's Christmas, sir, I grant you the season," McCawber boomed to Bob with a generous air and stately bow, although as he turned to admire some painting upon the wall, he muttered under his breath, "but my dear missus is ever the finest."

Mrs. Cratchit swept through the room, blowing each of her children air kisses, something Bob had never seen from his wife, who usually smothered anyone in sight with the friendly hug of a bear.

"Oh, Belinda, dear, that is ever so the most charming little bijou," she trilled, admiring a diamond necklace that was little only if compared to the Matterhorn.

"Oh, m'ma, you mean this adorable thing?" the girl affected right back. "I believe that it is from Mr. Chuzzlewit[20]."

---

[20] Martin Chuzzlewit.

Editor's note: Dickens created the dual characters of Martin Chuzzlewit senior and junior specifically to annoy his publisher. Indeed, Joseph Bunderston was thoroughly confused by two characters both named Martin Chuzzlewit and kept sending Dickens notes for clarification, which Dickens largely ignored except on occasion to befuddle him further. The very next year, Dickens even wrote the novel, The Life and Adventures of Martin Chuzzlewit, solely to

"Would that be Martin, junior, or senior?"

"You know, m'ma, I'm not sure I even recall. They both pay me such attentions that I give it no mind." And she laughed with a toss of her hair, and then held up the necklace so that it glimmered in the light. "I care only for matters that matter."

Bob Cratchit looked closer to make sure the girl was indeed his daughter. "This doesn't sound like my Belinda. Two men at the once, father and son both, concern only for jewels? Tell me it's not so."

"Well, sir, no, it is not so." McCawber hesitated, as Bob breathed a sigh of relief. "There are more than just a mere two men with whom she's courting her time."

Cratchit felt weak in the knees. It was all so strange he didn't know whether to laugh or cry, though crying had the early lead.

"Yes, well, sir, you knows the way of the young. Their ideas are their own, and never you say. Your Belinda, she just decided that poverty was not going to be her way."

Peter took out a large cigar from the humidor, and lit it with a one-pound note.

(*cont'd*) infuriate his publisher all the more – creating a well-to-do, though ever-suspicious grandfather and his more reckless but equally stubborn grandson who travels alone to America. To compound the very-intentional confusion beyond even this, Dickens used a title virtually identical to his novel, The Life and Adventures of Nicholas Nickleby.

Poverty? Cratchit couldn't understand what the Spirit was referring to. "There's no poverty here. There is money to...well, burn." Then a curious look crossed his face. "Where did all this money come from, anyway?"

"Ah. I was a-wondering when you might ask that," McCawber sighed.

"Is this something I should sit down for?" creaked Bob.

"I would say it might be better to lie flat on the floor."

As McCawber related, when eldest son Peter saw the firm faltering, he got his father to make him co-owner of Scrooge & Marley, to bring in newer, younger business. Instead, Peter approached Defarge & Dawkins and sold them the firm's billings for which he personally got most generous terms. He also received a sizeable finder's fee from D&D, and profits. Scrooge & Marley was soon after liquidated.

Bob dropped upon the sofa and at least landed near the youthful innocence of his two youngest, who were throwing a pillow back and forth at the other. "Being with them gives me a brief solace, I must admit," Cratchit said, as pillows went whipping by him. "The simple guilessness of their ways gives one a smile, at least on occasion."

"Oh, dear," McCawber averred. "Oh, dear, oh, me, oh, my. Thems young ones as what were young once did grow. And times were hard."

Cratchit looked at his two youngest, now fast asleep, though he wondered why "fast asleep" should be the description rather than slow asleep, for there is nothing nimble about lying in a lump unconscious. "Not these two, McCawber? They're far too uncomplicated," he said, using a fatherly expression rather than one currently in popular use for nervous disorders.

"With no money to be had, they were reduced to running about in the street," McCawber related carefully. "One day, a lorry hit them and, though not hurt, being used to crashing into walls, the driver thought otherwise and offered a large payment so as to avoid court. These young ones came upon the idea of feigning injury within traffic and being paid for it. And paid well, I might add and will add and do add. They are amongst the wealthiest and most bruised in all of London for their age."

It was impressive how a man tired as Cratchit could leap in vexation. It was with clenched eyes that he watched the two seeming-angels yet again race around the room. Martha presently grabbed them and boxed their ears for knocking over two Ming vases, and then hugged them for being such dears, bringing forth several "Hurrah, Martha's."

"Well, I must say I approve of her giving them a never-you-mind," Bob breathed in relief. "Clearly, Martha has grown into a wonderful mother and learned well from having her own."

The Ghost seemed like he wanted to be anywhere else but there at that instant and looked heavenward. Then he fluffed a cushion and signaled the spot to Cratchit to sit.

"No, not Martha?!" Bob's voice croaked out.

"When times went bad…"

Bob let out a long, low gurgle of agony that sounded like a cross between a high gurgle of agony and an especially low gurgle of agony, and put his hands to his head.

"...she was in tough straits, she was. So, she trained her three little ones to do a child family act for the stage, against their wishes. They met with the greatest success across Europe, but being minors, all their money is owned by her as guardian, and she only remits them but a few shillings. It is her personal fortune, and has not to feed or raise or even see her lonely, sad children, living herself in ease and majestic prosperity."

For the longest while, the Spirit thought he had killed Cratchit, as the gentleman didn't move. Afraid to find out, he could only watch, asking, "Cratchit? Cratchit, old man?" At last, he saw an eyebrow twitch, and knew all was well. Not so well for Bob, of course, but at least the Ghost knew was not on the line for causing any harm.

"Come, my children, the feast is before us," the matriarch intoned, while Rose carried a tray so huge the servant stumbled several times, though no one lent a hand.

"Could I have someone come here to cut my turkey!" Peter called to the kitchen.

"We're short of staff tonight," Belinda snorted. "Though it's our holiday, too!."

Martha nodded through clenched teeth. "And they'll expect to be paid for the day. A poor excuse for picking a man's pocket every twenty-fifth of December."

"Hurrah, Martha, hurrah!" the young ones cried, the boy trying to ingest his potato by sticking it in his ear.

"Their mother, why hasn't their mother stepped in to offer rebuke of anyone?" Cratchit finally blurted out.

The Ghost tried to figure how best to answer, then

thought better of it, shrugged and started to walk out of the room. When Cratchit realized, he called him back. "Oh, no, not this time," McCawber replied, "Get some other Spectre for this one."

"Spirit, come back. You are here to teach me."

"I was at home, having a wonderful Christmas with my dear Mrs. McCawber, I was, I didn't ask for this, says I. No, thank you very much."

"McCawber, please. Tell me of my wife. You'd want to know of your own dear missus."

It was a plea the Ghost couldn't ignore. "Look around." He waved at the large chamber, the many rooms off it, marble hallways, three fireplaces, the extensive grounds outside. "Did you not wonder where this opulent mansion came from?"

"Oh," Cratchit paused a moment. "No, I did not."

"Did you not perhaps wonder where you are in this picture?"

"Oh," he paused, realizing. "No, I did not."

McCawber again headed straight for the door. "I do not need to do this."

"Please, McCawber. God save the Queen. Rule Britannia. Cry God for Harry and England. I say, old chap. Hip, hip, hurrah. And all that."

Once more, the Ghost stopped. "An Englishman stands up for another Englishman. Even when one of them is deceased," and came back to do his duty.

As McCawber started to speak, Cratchit interrupted, "When my firm shut down and we were poor...Yes, yes, I know all that. What happened next??"

"Your good wife divorced you," the Ghost started, deeply sad to deliver the news, though sure to make clear it was Cratchit's good wife who had left, not McCawber's far better lady. "While you had no money, however, I'm most happy to tell you, I am, that there was a great deal of insurance on the company. So, good for you, I say, old chap! Alas, that lasted only 'til the settlement. But you can rest knowing that your good wife," and he again added sarcastic emphasis upon those two words, "was left well-cared for."

"All this came as results of my divorce?" Cratchit moaned, barely able to get out that detestable word.

"Oh, no. Not to worry. In truth, sir, in fact, sir, the whole family combined their provisions, knowing that jointly, oh, my, they would be quite the potent force, indeed, sir. Even my dear, good, great, gracious wife Mrs. McCawber," he let that sink in, "says as much about such things."

Cratchit looked upon his family at the table, not knowing these people he knew so well. "Oy," he drawled, using a colorful phrase he had overheard from Fagin that seemed especially appropriate right then.

Looking at his family, however, a thought pierced him. And if things couldn't get worse, they just did. "You said the family was together. Yet where is Tall Tim? Please, Spirit, tell me that in the future yet to be that he did not...that he did not..."

"Die?" McCawber asked.

And just then, the door to the mansion opened, and who should walk in but Tall Tim himself! "Walk in" may not be the correct phrase, however, as hobbled would be more accurate, given the leg braces strapped to his limbs and crutches he carried.

"Thank you, <u>Lady Dedlock</u>[21]," the young man cried out to a neighbour, "your good wishes and charity are beyond kind, especially on this of all days. A blessing upon your house."

Cratchit was overjoyed to find that his son had not…that word…though saddened to see that Tim's old illness had returned. He deserved so much better, that fine lad.

The young man tossed the crutches into a corner and tore off the braces, striding to join the others, sniggering, "And don't just put a blessing upon it, you cheap crone, but a new coat of paint, as well. That's the bleakest house to fit a bleak old woman."

---

[21] Lady Dedlock.

Editor's note: Though Lady Dedlock is unseen here as nothing more than being mentioned as a next-door neighbor, Dickens somehow became intrigued by her home which is referred to in a way he felt intriguingly cryptically, though to most scholars it seems fairly straight forward. Because he wanted to know more about the Lady and where she lived, however, Dickens made her the mysterious grand dame of his subsequent novel Bleak House, who holds secrets about her secret past secretively. Between these many bleak secrets, and her bleak name "Dedlock" and the title <u>Bleak House</u>, it wasn't Dickens at his most subtle.

Cratchit turned to the Ghost. "I'm not going to want to see this, am I?"

The family greeted Tall Tim with hugs all around. Peter poured his brother a large whiskey. "How was it, Tim? Have the coffers been filled?"

"Ah, begging is always a good business, but this time of year, oh, yes!" he smiled the biggest smile you could ever imagine for so ignoble a purpose. Emptying his pockets, money cascaded onto the table. "It certainly doesn't hurt to remind them upon Christmas Day who made lame beggars walk and blind men see," and he laughed that hearty laugh that brought a smile to all who heard it, except his father at the moment.

There was a pounding at the door, and Tim quickly put down his glass. "Bless my soul, I forgot my partner." He soon came back helping a crippled young man, his body twisted and fingers bent, walking slowly with a measured limp.

"Rest yourself, Smike[22]," Mrs. Cratchit proffered, " a seat

---

[22] Smike.

From the publisher's notes: "Mr. Dickens, A question if I may. Why in the world have you chosen to use the character of Smike yet again in this story? I cannot imagine that readers will not remember he had been in The Life and Adventures of Nicholas Nickleby a mere four years ago. After all, you so memorably portrayed him and heartbreakingly so as the poor unfortunate young man who Nicholas rescues from the Dotheboys institute." To this letter, a shocked and truly-embarrassed Dickens wrote of honor for a friend of the feast."

"To my dear partner," Tall Tim cried out, raising his glass, "I praise the day I saw you begging in the park. You were an artist! And an even greater success."

"It were nothing, one does what one has to, to survive," the lame fellow replied very slowly, as he filled his plate.

'What you taught me, I can never repay. Nor do I intend to, ha ha!" Tim laughed and slapped his friend on the back. "After a   childhood taunted as 'Mr. Crutch-it,' it was Providence's great revelation that I could use my past to build our futures, everyone! To organize the crippled, feeble and poor citizenry of London – and those clever folk who pretend to appear so," he added with a wink that brought gales of laughter, oh, such were the happy feelings there, "and run a business from it. So, again, I wish you the season!"

"To Smike!" everybody cried.

"Thank you," he stated. "Might someone please pass the pudding?"

"Tell me, Spirit," Bob said, after he finally had the spirit, "that this is not the future that will be, that it is not even the future that can be, that it is only the shadow as like a fevered

---

(*cont'd*) back, "I did?! I had no idea! I saw some notes I had written about the character lying about and thought they were meant for this book. Oh, well, that means readers get him a second time. Given that the character was so memorable, as you say, then I suppose the public are the lucky ones to have him return." Bunderston pointedly wrote back, "By the way, Smike died."

dream where all our worst fears reside, the unspoken terrors that leave us shaken in the utter horror of our failings that drive men to silent despair in the darkest hours."

The Ghost came close to Cratchit with a soft expression upon its visage, putting its hand's upon Bob's shoulder and making certain they had one another's attention.

"Look on the bright side, sir," McCawber intoned. "The bright side, says I. Things could be worse, sir. Never forget that. Things could always be worse."

Cratchit laughed to himself, not of humour, but at the impasse upon which he found himself, for which a chortle seemed the only release. "Worse, yes. And how would that be?

Suddenly, the Spirit stopped, and looked as if it had been following a horse-and-buggy and had stepped in one of the gifts left behind. It quickly tried to change Bob's attention and divert the conversation elsewhere. "Oh, my," it said, scouring the walls in a pose of actually being interested, "is that painting an original?" And then, concerned that Cratchit was not distracted, added, "Would you like to see a trick?" and grabbed a handkerchief from its pocket.

A look of understanding crossed Cratchit's visage. "Spirit, what could be worse? Tell me. Tell me."

"Who's to say what will happen? As you yourself point out, this could be just a bad, frightening dream." Then it waved its hands and made eerie ghost sounds, "Ooooo."

"Tell me." And in an instant, the realization occurred to Cratchit. "Me. It's about me. The terrible thing as could happen." For once, McCawber was silent. "I have been through much since the first visit of your fellow Spirits. I wish to see more."

The Ghost was reticent to comply, but at last he motioned the trembling Cratchit to follow. Thinking they were entering the parlor, Bob warily passed under the transom and found himself instead in a large graveyard under the cover of night, where his shaky legs stumbled, and he fell to the ground.

Almost too concerned to speak, Bob found his voice and asked where they were and what he was to find here.

The Ghost did not answer. Instead, he stood silently before a gravestone and with his arm raising, pointed with a flourish to the writing etched on it. With trepidation, Cratchit crawled over. He lifted his eyes and read. Then, he turned to the Spirit –

"I'm sorry, I don't recognize the name."

McCawber leaned over and peered at the writing. "That's not right. It's not this one at all. No, it's…" and once more, he dramatically pointed. A crash of lightning shone on the words, surprising Cratchit because the night was clear. He read the stone.

Again, Bob threw his hands out to the Wraith. "I'm sorry, I just don't know who in the world this person is."

"Oh, stuff and bother, all these headstones look alike, and the dark don't make it easier. You don't have a torch, do you?" McCawber stumbled around the cemetery, peering at markers, putting on spectacles, and then gave up. "Oh, never no mind, what it says somewhere here is 'William Sikes. A good man, better father and bestest grandfather ever. Gracious in his soul, he will be missed.'

"Bill Sikes? Certainly, there must be some mistake," Cratchit stammered, now pretty much settled in a state of bewilderment. "Perhaps it's another by the same name."

"No, that's the Bill Sikes. And before I came here tonight he asked me to remind you that you still owe his employer and 'not to forget to pays up whens you gets back.'"

"How did he change into such a great person?"

"Oh, he didn't change. He just got rich. So good at his work bullying people that he got hired as head of security at Defarge & Dawkins. Retired with an obscene amount of money. The fellow's an absolute disaster as a human being, oh, my, yes. Horrible, horrible," and then McCawber shrugged. "But anyhowever, it's all very simple. Die wealthy, and you'll be loved. Die poor and live alone."

"But what does any of this have to do with me?" It was a humbling experience for Cratchit. But not so humbling as when another bolt of lighting crashed, and he was now standing outside a ramshackle tenement of many flats and rotted wood.

A broken door to one of the flats was unable to close, as McCawber led the way in for Cratchit. The place was closer to a spacious closet than room. Seated in back was an old, wrinkled fellow, decrepit as a hollowed-out man could be, almost more wraith than the actual Wraith near him. His white hair thinned to reveal a nearly-smooth pate.

Cratchit was much saddened, yet surprised to find that he felt better for himself at the moment, seeing another in such a worse plight, and so mentioned to McCawber that he now understood why he was brought here. "But who is the poor, old miserable creature? Wait, is that Mr. Scrooge??!" he asked in full shock.

"No! That is not me!" Scrooge bellowed, as he suddenly materialized next to Bob, as if out of thin air, which is pretty much where he did come from, and as red in the face as a pale ghost is able to get, livid. "First, you think I'm fat as Father Christmas, and now you think I'm as decrepit as a decomposed old tree rotted upon the ground. No, that is not me! You saw me but recently. Did I look like that? Have you gone daft, man?"

"Then, who…?"

"It's you, Cratchit! That is you! For goodness sake."

Clearly, there was no goodness about it, as Cratchit made sure his sight was not impaired. "Me? So old I am. How many years have I been in this execrable place?"

"Old?," Scrooge almost laughed. "This is three years from the present." He then added, without necessity, "The intervening time has not been kind to you."

Cratchit circled the figure in the chair, who was eating a bowl of dishwater, flavoured with a few pieces of tree bark. This could not be himself, he was sure of it.

""Good King Wenceslas la la," the withered chap began to sing, "at the feet of Stephen."

"At the feast of Stephen! Feast!" Scrooge bellowed, "'Good King Wenceslas went out at the feast of Stephen.' Can't you even get the words right after all these years, man? For goodness sake!" He turned to McCawber, tossing his arms up, "I leave him to you, if I stay with the fellow any longer I might wash my hands of the whole affair."

And with that, Scrooge was gone. Yet again.

"Bless my soul, such tasty stew," Old Cratchit croaked, as he sipped the thin liquid. "If only, though, I could afford a sprinkle of salt. Never no mind."

It was a piteous sight, and Cratchit didn't know who to feel worse for – himself or himself. All he could think of was a rich and honored Bill Sikes and Mr. Scrooge when they died, and himself alive, poor and alone.

"There's always that 'bright side' suggestion of mine," the Ghost repeated. "Though you may be in the corner on this here one. Still, as I always say, if you're sitting in a pub with your health, you don't need a shilling in your pocket, so long as you have a friend who owns the pub."

Whilst they were talking, Old Cratchit had put on his threadbare coat, wrapped a threadbare scarf around his neck, and put on a threadbare hat. They followed him as he left the threadbare flat, trudging the snowy streets, wheezing, and getting badly lost several times, occasionally ending up where he had started, before finally continuing on his deliberate, painful, pathetic way.

"Do you know where he – where I – am headed, Spirit?"

"Indeed, sir, I do, indeed."

"Could we not have just met there and waited?" Cratchit inquired, becoming a bit tired at this point, not to mention irritable.

"Ah, but then, sir you'd not have seen the image of what your life had become. The getting lost, turning the wrong way, going in circles."

"You dragged me along on this interminable walk solely as a metaphor?"

"I wouldn't use that word exactly, no, sir, I wouldn't."

"Well, what was it then?"

"Oh, it was that, I'm sure. I just wouldn't use the word. Oh, ha, here were are."

They had come to a corner that led into a large square. The Cathedral of Defarge and Dawkins loomed ahead.

"You arrive here each day, hoping to find work," McCawber explained. "But not a soul will take you on, ever. O such a deplorable failure of society. Mind you, given your past history of business failure, it's understandable. It's a sad sight, though. Let's go see it."

There ahead was a sea of other lost souls, each adrift in unanswered hopes, their bodies filling the plaza. And into this wave upon wave of nameless faces and equally nameless necks and arms and legs walked Old Cratchit, no longer Old Cratchit but yet another nameless face and nameless assorted body parts, indeed not even that any more but swallowed by the sea of multitudes as it bled into an ocean and the ocean poured across the land.

"Oh, my, that's a bad go," said McCawber. "I could be as wrong, of course, as it's your life. But still, to me, to my way of thinking, this is not an ideal future yet to be."

Nor was it to Cratchit's way of thinking. It was a ghastly sight, this future he was looking at. He fell to the ground, writhing in agony and the snow.

"Oh, Spirit, I will not be the man of the past I was in the future. What I mean is, in the past, the man I was will not be that same man in the future who I'll become. And while I know that no man is ever precisely the same in the future exactly from what they were in the past, for the change of even a single day is change itself, I will be more different still."

The Ghost looked around, hoping that no one was able to see this very un-English display of feelings, and of course no one was, yet he still moved a few steps away so as not to be associated with it, just to make certain.

"I wish to change, Spirit. I wish to be a different man. I wish to see a different future yet to be. Grant me this, Spirit. Grant me this."

"Well, I would very much like to," McCawber said, scratching his head awkwardly, "but I fear you have mistaken me for a genie. That's a different kind of spirit entirely, you see, and usually entails a lamp of some sort."

Cratchit moved quickly towards the Ghost, much swifter than it thought a man on his knees could move, and therefore was unable to get away before Cratchit grabbed hold of McCawber's leg.

"I have the teachings of all the three Spirits in my heart. I have learned the lessons of the Ghosts of Christmas Past, Present and Yet to Be, or whatever it is you wished to be called, and will carry those with me for all my days. And all of my nights, as well, even when I sleep, for I know that that is when spirits seem to like to lurk around. Oh, Spirit – Spirits – thank you for your graces, and let me have a chance to live what you taught me, so that this future I see in the present will be a thing of the past."

As Cratchit held all the tighter upon McCawber's leg, the Ghost dragged him around the sidewalk attempting to loosen him, but to no avail. Finally in a secluded spot, he let the man have his say, for McCawber was anything if not polite, and as soon as he felt Cratchit had finished, or at least when Cratchit had stopped to take a breath, the Ghost vanished. And Cratchit found that he was clutching a pillow.

Stave Five

THE BEGINNING OF THE END LEADING DIRECTLY TO THE END OF THE END WHICH MAY BE A NEW BEGINNING

How in heaven's name a pillow could be found lying in a city square at that moment is a mystery of the age, but there a pillow was and in the hands of Cratchit. When the gentleman in question stopped to think about it, however, he realized that since the plaza was now a destination for the homeless, many had brought small comforts. It was thus that the pillow found its way there, Cratchit was certain.

Bob moved quickly to find whence the Spirit may have gone, but all he found was a patch of ice from which his foot went flying, the rest of his body along with it. Together, they landed in a large snowdrift. When finally he pushed himself out, he was back in his own bed with his head sticking out of his own sheets.

Home! He was home, Bob Cratchit was. And dry and warm and happy. At first he didn't know how happy he was for he was too happy to think of it. But soon, the sunlight streaming in, and seeing his room exactly as he remembered it, except that the drawer where he kept his pocket watch was open, he began bouncing upon his bed and knew how happy he was.

Home! Oh, what a glorious word and even more glorious a place. Cratchit leapt off of the bed and leapt into the hallway and leapt and leaped and then even jumped too and skipped once though he always looked silly skipping, and then leapt some more, knocking over a prized vase that had been on a table.

Oh, my, the missus will not be pleased about that, he thought. "I'll blame it on the dog!" he said out loud, until recalling that the family had no dog but instead would blame it on a crosswind, realizing that not only would this take blame off himself, but he could also collect an indemnity covering its protection against acts of nature. And this made Cratchit happier still, for it was not an idea he would have had before, which meant he was carrying on the lessons he learned from the Spirits, as he pledged.

"I am happy, euphoric, glad, joyous, light-headed, mirthful!" he cried out loud, naming all the words he could think of that were appropriate and unsure why he was speaking out loud, except that he was so jubilant, "Oh, there's another one, jubilant!" he shouted out loud. Cratchit was jolly as St. Nicholas, merry as Christmas and nutty as a fruitcake.

116

Everything took on new meaning to Bob, especially that for which he had never placed much value. The china dishes, magnificent, and worth a pretty penny. The magnificent chest of drawers that was a magnificent antique and all the more magnificently valuable for it. He had so much that was priceless in his life – and in his home. What a magnificent thing to discover.

"The day!" Cratchit realized. He had no idea what day it was, or even the time. Passing a clock, he saw that it was 9:47, so that answered that, "But I still don't know the day," and laughed at the pure excitement of being alive. He ran to the window overlooking the street and pulled it open.

O what a glorious day it was! Snow everywhere, and the sun glistening off it like little diamonds. Sweet sights, sweet smells, sweet sounds, the nearby clack of a wheelbarrow, its owner selling cockles and mussels, alive, alive, oh, Cratchit was alive and felt as glorious as the day itself.

A man wearing a heavy coat and tall hat passed by underneath, and Cratchit called to him, at last having an excuse to speak out loud.

"Halloo! What's today?!" he shouted.

"I beg your pardon? Today?" the man replied, bewildered, after looking around for the disembodied voice. "Who's that? It's December 28."

"You're quite sure?? The 28th? Not Christmas Day? You're certain?"

"I did not forget three days, no," snapped the gentleman. "Of course, I'm certain, or my name isn't Chuzzlewit."

"Well, it must be so, then, for I…" Cratchit stopped.

"Chuzzlewit did you say? Martin Chuzzlewit?"

"Do I know you, sir?"

"Martin, the senior, or junior?"

"Why, junior, it is. Have we met?"

"Get out!" Cratchit yelled. "Leave of this instant before I call a constable on you! And stay away from my daughter, or I will give you what for, sir."

"Your daughter? I don't know her, I'm sure."

"And you make certain you keep it that way in the future yet to be, Chuzzlewit, and your father, too. I'll be watching. Again. Be gone!" And gone he was.

December the 28th, Cratchit thought, well, that makes sense. It would take three days at the very least for the Spirits to do all that work. If he missed Christmas this year, then so be it, as far as Cratchit was concerned it was the best Christmas present – as well as best Christmas past and Christmas yet to be. He laughed, "I do love that joke."

There was a noise out the window, and thinking it might be that Chuzzlewit again with perhaps his whole brood, Cratchit returned with a shotgun, but it turned out instead to be a child of around fifteen. An idea came to him.

"Hallo! Young boy down there. A word with you."

"You mean me?!" the cry came back.

"Oh, a lovely boy, a delightful lad, such a pleasure to speak to. Yes, boy, you!"

"I'm not a boy. I'm a girl."

"Oh, of course, you are a boy. I can see with my own

eyes. A charming lad, a pleasant lad, though an argumentative one."

"On my word, sir, I wouldn't lie about such a thing." She removed her cap, and her dark curls tumbled out." "See, I'm a girl. Florence Dombey[23]"

"Oh, a sweet girl, a darling girl," Cratchit sang out, as everything was wonderful in his eyes. If a tidal wave just then swept over the town of Folkstone, he would probably have found something adorable about it. "Tell me, girl, do you know Bill Sikes?"

"What? The fellow as big as a mountain? I should say I

---

[23] Florence Dombey.

Editor's note: Dickens was intrigued by the idea he wrote here of a little girl confused for a boy. He made notes for this, and years later this was somewhat the idea behind his novel, Dombey and Son. In that, Florence Dombey's father always wanted to have a son, even naming his firm as such, but gets a daughter instead. The publisher was extremely upset when he received the finished novel, having been told to expect a book called Dombey and Son and finding that there was no "son" at all, but rather that the story was about Dombey and daughter. Bunderston and Dickens were no longer speaking in person at this point, though the publisher wrote to his author, "Dear sir, I am checking with our firm's solicitors as to whether this is a cause for breach of contract or misrepresentation." Eventually, the threat of a lawsuit was dropped.

do. Not personally, of course, thank the Lord. But of him."

"A bright girl. A perceptive lass. Go and find him, and tell him to meet me at noon at the spot he and I last spoke, and if you're back here in half an hour I will give you five shillings."

"No, thank you," she said, backing off. "I want nothing to do with Bill Sikes."

"Four shillings, then."

"No, not even if you…" Miss Dombey stopped, a look of confusion over her face. "Before, you had said five shillings."

"So, I did," Cratchit acknowledged, "and each moment that goes by, the price will go down. Three shilling six. Three shillings," the amount shrinking as his new-found business acumen grew, "two shillings six."

"I'll take it!" she cried, unhappy at having to find Sikes, but unwilling to risk the price plummeting further. She raced off to earn her reward.

"I'm so giddy, I don't know what to do," Cratchit thought, but then he smiled, "yes, I do know! And I know how to do it. And why. O what a wondrous plan! Thank you, Spirits, for making everything so clear to me."

He was already dressed, thanks to his foresight during his ghostly outing with Mr. Scrooge, so Cratchit had time in excess to ensure his plan was properly contrived, for thus organized was the new Bob. Presently, the young miss returned to report that Bill Sikes would meet him, and Bob gave her an extra sixpence for her efforts. It wasn't much at all, yet still unnecessary, but efficiency should be rewarded.

Leaving the house for his many duties ahead, he noticed that old knocker on the door, in the image of Mr. Scrooge. "I really must get that replaced," he said to himself.

As Cratchit headed through the snowy streets of London, he would greet passersby with a cheerful, "Merry three days after Christmas," eliciting curious looks, but it was no matter to Bob, for the world was a curious place. Oh, my, didn't he know better than anyone about that.

People he knew, he would go out of his way to greet, even following them down a cross street. "The good day to you," Bob would shout joyfully amidst a benevolent seasonal hug. "Don't forget that loan, it's coming due!" Surprised looks came from those seeing this brand-new Cratchit. He smiled a smile that made others smile back, and if ever a man could now give hearty handshakes, that man was Cratchit, "May your holiday season be joyous ever, and remember that we do hold the lien upon your property!"

Seeing a fellow who was but a day away from default and giving a shout, the gentleman must not have heard Cratchit above the seasonal noise, for he began racing away. Not wishing to lose even one new "good day," Bob gave chase. Reaching the blocked-end of an alley, the borrower noted indeed he hadn't heard Cratchit's yelling and then expressed concern that his creditor would foreclose upon him.

Cratchit brushed away such fears with a booming laugh, "As long as you meet your obligations, we will never foreclose. Never!"

"But what if I can't meet them?" the fellow meekly inquired.

"Worry not one whit!" shouted Cratchit with a happy cry. "Bob's your uncle, as our elders say, and so I am. We will work out new terms. Perhaps more favorable to us, but what is more favorable to you than having every chance to keep what's yours. We want you to succeed. It's why we exist. But if you want free money, I suggest you plant a forest of free money trees. Merry three days after Christmas!"

Bob continued on his merry way and stopped in at his church. He apologized to the pastor for missing the service upon Christmas Day, sure that the sermon had been a most wondrous one about faith, decency and brotherhood, and added that he would deliver his New Year's contribution in a few days hence, but to expect only half as much as the previous year.

At last, Cratchit reached his true destination, a large house in the wealthiest part of town. Ushered into the sitting room, his apprentice Mr. Twist soon arrived with a look upon his face that couldn't have been more surprised by any visitor. Cratchit offered that he had come here privately since he didn't wish to make his offer known in the public view of the office.

"The firm has been closed since Christmas Eve, sir, three days past. No one knew where you have been. It's good see you well." What Twist was thinking, though, was that it was especially good to see his employer alive.

Cratchit got down to business, and business it was that he wished to discuss. "The firm of Scrooge & Marley is in a dire state. No need for you to deny it on my account." Twist had made no such effort, and would not have thought of doing so. "I fear that unless a significant change is made, we may be forced to shut down."

Rather than being concerned, young Twist was delighted that Mr. Cratchit was actually facing the crisis, something he thought as likely as the moon inviting him to tea.

"Therefore, Mr. Twist, as I know you are a bright man of business, a good man of business, a fine man of business, an impressive man of business, in short," (though it was long past that possibility at this point) "a businessman of business, I wish to propose you join me as junior partner."

If Oliver Twist could have been more astonished, he couldn't have been more astonished. If he could have spoken, he would have said that he was speechless. Cratchit explained that he saw the hardworking Twist as a fellow of many plans, aggressive in accomplishing them, and someone able to bring unexplored funds into the firm.

When the young man finally found his voice, which as it turned out was right where he had left it, he said that it was timely that Mr. Cratchit should bring this up now, as he had just been going over such plans with a Mr. Nickleby, who was waiting at that very moment in another room.

"Bless my soul, I had no idea," said Cratchit, who had every idea that a Mr. Nickleby would be here, having overheard it when Bob was a shadowed party guest the night before. "Do bring him in, please."

When Twist returned with Nicholas Nickleby[24], the latter

---

[24] Nicholas Nickleby.

Editor's note: Four years earlier, Dickens had written The Life and Adventures of Nicholas Nickleby, the expansive tale of a good-hearted young man trying to make his way in the world, quashed repeatedly for no particular reason by his mean-spirited, rich uncle. When he dropped the young man into this story, Dickens quickly received a harsh, blunt explained as how he'd recently come into a fortune upon the death of an uncle, and was looking to invest. Cratchit said he was sorry to hear of the loss, and meant it, but he also felt that as long as Mr. Nickleby was going to lose a relative, it might as well be a wealthy one. The young gentleman thanked his well-wisher, and meant it, but he also felt that as long as one was going to lose a relative, it might as well be a cruel, thoughtless and vindictive one.

The three good souls got along famously and found that their ideas for the future held much in common. Cratchit saw the lengthening time and explained that he had an appointment elsewhere, suggesting they meet that very afternoon to start their plan in motion, and begged their leave.

"By all means, sir," Nickleby replied with kindness, "and I can safely say that our interests soon will be such that that will be the last thing you ever beg for again."

(*cont'd*) letter from Bunderston. "Sir, why in heavens name have you taken so pronounced and vibrant a character as Mr. Nickelby and given him an almost-insignificant role in this little tale, for no particular reason? It reeks of desperation at best, and a lack of creativity at worst. Please consider changing this." Dickens didn't, as his intent on using Nicholas Nickleby in this Christmas story was to be a play on words with "St. Nicholas," something he was sure readers would grasp and heartily enjoy, and was appalled that the publisher had not. Not surprisingly, he also took some offense at the publisher's words, and several acrimonious letters back-and-forth ensued.

Little sunlight ever found its way into the back alley where Cratchit anxiously waited for Bill Sikes. When the brute of a man finally arrived, he stomped over to Cratchit, and with his forefinger pushed Bob back several steps. "I 'opes you 'aves the money 'ere, Cratchit. I don't likes to be dragged about for no reason, I don't."

"And who would, Mr. Sikes?! Indeed, the money do I have. Here it all is, and a little something extra for you. Buy something nice for the children." He was a great deal of money, but knew it would be repaid in benefits many times over.

Sikes didn't know what to make of this. No one had ever given him a gratuity before. "Thankee," he was able to say, and then realized, "tho' I ain't got no children."

"Well, keep up hope, I'm sure some lucky lass is bound to come your way," Bob encouragingly patted the tough on the shoulder. "But no matter, I'm here on another matter. I would like to hire you to work for me. " He handed a paper to Sikes, "This is a list of people in serious default and their home addresses. Be kind, but most firm. And anything you can collect, Mr. Sikes, eight percent do you yourself get to keep."

Bill Sikes had never heard such generosity towards himself. And to be given an incentive, to have his own worth be given value, it was unlike anything he had felt in his life, and a tear came to his eye. "Yes, Mr. Cratchit, sir, it would be as a pleasure to work for yer, sir. Thankee, sir, and I will do me best, you just see as if I don't."

"Do your job well, Mr. Sikes, because there is a great future ahead for all of us."

With that, he left the very tall man standing taller than

before, with a new sense of pride and purpose. O the power of a kind word and the promise of great income.

When later that afternoon Cratchit arrived outside Defarge's, not yet a cathedral, nor partnered yet with Dawkins, but the same coarse office as just days before, Twist and Nickleby were already anxiously awaiting him.

"Are you ready, gentlemen?" Cratchit inquired. "For many of our future plans rely on success here today."

The offices were busy as ever, and the three callers ("the three wise men" Cratchit liked to consider them, though he kept that to himself) made their way through the rush of bodies over to where sat Jack Dawkins. Cratchit cleared his throat and with a silent admonition of "Courage!" to himself, directed Mr. Dawkins attention to himself.

"Not now, Mr. Cratchit, as you can see I'm very busy," the chap snapped dismissively, "though I can understand as how you wouldn't recognize such a condition."

"It is important that we talk, Mr. Dawkins, on a matter of business."

"What? Do you want to stuff even more money in my hand for no apparent reason?" the manager laughed, recalling their encounter Christmas Eve. "For if you do, I..." Dawkins's eyes suddenly flew wide open in recognition. "Twist? Is that you?!"

Oliver starred back closely, and his face lit up, as well. "Oh, my! I recognized the name Jack Dawkins, but I never realized it was one and the same. "Dodger!" He spun to Bob. "Mr. Cratchit, this is my old mate the Artful Dodger!

Oliver wrapped his distant friend in a hug so close as like

to squeeze the air out of him. Admiringly, he ran his hands along the fancy tailored lapel of Dawkins's coat, "Oh, my, aren't you a respectable old gentleman, you are." And hugged him once more.

"Mr. Twist. I must insist," Cratchit admonished him harshly. "If we are to continue with our partnership in mutual benefit, you must behave professionally."

Jack Dawkins let out a laugh. "Partners? Ha ha ha! Well, don't go building a new home for yourself just yet, Oliver. Any venture with Cratchit here is not likely to last, if you get my meaning," something it was unlikely for anyone to miss.

"All well and good, Mr. Dawkins, but we have come to make an offer to buy out this company. Mr. Nickleby here," Bob noted, and Nicholas nodded, "is providing sufficient funds which, with others available at our disposal, should prove quite enough."

For a moment, Dawkins could only stare at the three men before him. At last, the heartiest, most uproarious guffaw burst forth from his depths. "Oh! You're serious!" And he laughed and laughed and laughed again, long and loud.

An old crotchety French voice broke through the bustling noise of the room. "Mr. Dawkins, what is the meaning of this interruption?" Madame Defarge carried her knitting over to the disturbance.

Through his tears of mirth, Dawkins explained what had transpired, and though laughter was not part of her constitution, the old woman did emit a loud snort and scornful glance, which for her was as close to laughter as possible, and ordered the intruders out. The three insisted they wouldn't leave until their offer was met.

"And why would I consider selling my firm to anyone? Most especially..." and she gave them a withering glare – all in all, a more common aspect of her constitution – "...to you?"

If you had careful eyes, you might have noticed the expression on Bob Cratchit's face change ever so slightly. Even without careful eyes, you might have noticed it, though the chances would have been less likely, hence the benefit of careful eyes. It was an expression leaning towards great pleasure, though doing its best to remain at calm.

"The question is not why should you sell to anyone, Madame. The reason you should sell to us is because if you don't, the law will be interested in reading the contents of this."

Mr. Twist pulled from his jacket the paper Dawkins had hidden so carefully inside his coat the day Cratchit and Scrooge's ghost were there as shadows and saw. Dawkins quickly searched his inside pocket, and when the sheet was nowhere to be found – other than in Cratchit's hand – a frantic glance crossed the faces of Dawkins and Defarge.

"How did you get that!" Dawkins choked

"Mr. Twist just handed it to me."

"I could see that, you goose. What I mean..."

"I know what you meant," it was Cratchit's turn to drip with sarcasm, and he enjoyed the experience. "I'm not completely foolish. How we got it was very simple."

Oliver stood there, a wide grin that only stopped from exceeding the limits of his face by the fortunate advent of his ears, and his fingers wriggled lightly in the air. "'Oh, what a respectable gentleman you are, indeed,'" he mimicked himself.

"You picked my pocket when we hugged?? Dawkins sputtered. "Twist, how could you?!"

"How could I not? It's a crime to let one's old skills wither from disuse, as Mr. Cratchit suggested to me," he replied (thinking, too, that it was a wonder how in the world Mr. Cratchit knew of his long-buried past). "Besides, Jack, you and this woman here are causing great hurt to others, and doing so unfairly. We want to run an honest business of aid and growth and responsibility and various other good and noble things."

Madame Defarge croaked with much bluster that this was blackmail and demanded the paper be returned, but there was not nearly as much bluster as she wished, which was a great deal.

"Not blackmail," said Cratchit calmly. "We are prepared to make you a generous, fully-legitimate offer that is more than the value of your firm. Mind you, I suspect that at best this paper would raise many questions with those in authority about the practices here. At worst…" and he shrugged at Dawkins, "I wouldn't build a new home for yourself just yet. If you get my meaning," trying out that dripping-with-sarcasm idea once again, and beginning to enjoy it very much.

"It is stolen," the woman repeated, thunderingly.

"Now there you may have us," Cratchit acknowledged. "It's a dubious point, though, as we will claim we found in the office. Which actually we did. But if it concerns you, we're most happy to return it – right after I makes a copy."

"He's trained as a scrivener," Twist noted.

"What in the world is that?" Nickleby asked. Cratchit said

he'd try to explain later.

Madame Defarge was sullen. At long last, recognizing that making a profit was better than life in prison, she signaled that they join her in the back to sign.

With broad smiles, the three gentleman turned to one another and shook hands. Their future had just begun. The past a thing of the past. And if any man alive was an expert at the blending of the future and past in the present, that man was Bob Cratchit.

But he was early to the office the next morning. Oh, if he could only be first there, that was his one desire. Perhaps not his one desire. In fact, he didn't care especially if he was first, just that he beat Uriah Heep there, for he knew that Heep of all people would be most surprised by the changes at Scrooge & Marley's.

As it happened, Cratchit was first to the office, having arrived two hours early. By eight o'clock, he looked at the clock, and no Heep, not unexpected since no one was due for another hour, but you never could be sure. But his plan was in motion.

A quarter of an hour before nine, employees who had come by to see if the office would finally be open were particularly happy to see Mr. Cratchit, for that meant not only was he breathing, but that they still had jobs.

At five minutes to nine, there was no Uriah. Three minutes before the hour, still no Uriah. A full forty-five seconds before nine o'clock, in walked Uriah Heep.

Before the head clerk had even a chance to remove his hat from his oily head and unwrap his scarf from his oily neck,

Cratchit stepped up, surprising the oily fellow.

"Oh! Mr. Cratchit, sir, it's so good, sir, to see you, sir, and know, sir, that you are so well, sir, and have reopened, sir. I 'umbly wish you a Merry Christmas, sir, sir, sir."

"You really are quite an unctuous fellow, aren't you – sir?

"Sir?

"Sir, no need to remove your apparel. No need for you to take your place at your desk. No need for you to do anything but wait until I finish."

Heep was concerned at the tone of this, for it was not the employer he had gotten to know and gotten to get around. His eyes darted, and so, he thought, might he.

"Per'aps Mr. Cratchit still ain't as feeling well yet, and it's best that I 'umbly find a doctor for 'im."

Cratchit stepped in his path. "Pray don't leave. Others wish to make your acquaintance." And on that word, the door to his office flew open and out rushed an army of men, some who blocked the front exit (which could no longer be considered an exit), others who surrounded Heep with pistols drawn and knives and clubs. Constables there were, private investigators, as well, along with friends of Bill Sikes who that good chap had sent (himself busy earning his eight percent elsewhere), barristers to make certain all was handled in a legal manner, and the newest partner Mr. Twist.

The situation did not appear especially agreeable to Heep. He hunched even more than ever, something one would never have imagined possible.

And Bob Cratchit looked taller than ever. He addressed his soon-to-be-former head clerk in a voice strong for all the room to hear.

"There is one man of perfidy, and that man – HEEP – is he who is none other. There is one man – HEEP – who has himself – HEEP – lied, cheated and faked in every way imaginable and in many unimaginable. A man – HEEP – for whom in my hand I have the false records he kept that prove him – HEEP – to be the cheating, deceiving, villainous, thieving criminal that he – HEEP – is. And as far as treachery and falsehood go, there is no one more so than he – HEEP, HEEP, HEEP, HEEP, HEEP – himself.

How mortified Cratchit was that his great passion of the moment should manifest itself as hiccoughs. That everyone present believed him repeatedly calling out the name of his head clerk did not obscure that the world now knew Uriah Heep was a lying, thieving lowlife. For proof Bob Cratchit now had.

Uriah Heep scrambled to his desk, looking desperately for his forged ledgers, but they were gone, into the hand of Cratchit. He knew not how Cratchit could have learned their hiding place. But before even a word could escape the villainous den that was his mouth, Cratchit shouted, "Take him! Arrest him! Begone!" and the despicable lowlife was dragged out of the office.

Oh, my, Cratchit felt wonderful about that. Wonderful friends supporting him. Wonderful recovering money lost. Wonderful to aid society by seeing a thief in prison. Wonderful that thief rotting there, receiving what he deserved. Wonderful his being locked in with others so vicious, unable to sleep out of fear he might become their next victim„ a quivering mass of regret, lost in a dank, festering, pitiful cell. Wonderful thoughts, wonderful actions, won-der-ful retribution!

Seeing the smiling faces all around him, Cratchit announced his new partner to all, which brought forth shouts of cheers of "hurrah," loud celebrations and murmured whispers of "Twist? Did he say Twist was to be his new partner?" Then, he turned to the secretary and proclaimed, "Miss Havisham, lower the flames of the inferno burning in this stove, it's far too hot for man or beast. And do it before you cross another 't'!"

This brought forth shouts of blessed relief from his sweating staff. All, that is, but Miss Havisham, who stomped, "Before I make a pot of tea? It's not yet tea time. Do you take me for a heathen?"

Cratchit started to correct her, but put his arms around the lady in a hug, for in truth the truth is he felt much too wonderful.

Wonderful is how Bob Cratchit felt on his walk home. The road seemed more clear than ever before, just like his life. How kind the people were when he passed them this three days after Christmas, the good-will of the season continuing, even though most owed the firm money. "Good afternoon, Mr. Cratchit, sir!" "Did you lose weight, what a youthful step you have, take a piece of fruit, how do you stay so fit, that colour suits you so well, surely you must be Bob Cratchit's younger and more handsome brother."

If you know any man who could be in finer humour than Bob Cratchit, I should like to meet him, also. Tender an introduction, and I shall be forever in your debt, though debt unlike that owed Cratchit, I wish to be clear. Few men could be as full of mirth as that gentleman himself, heartily shaking the hands of all and noting how anxious they appeared at first, yet each breathed elation after he passed them by. Oh, if a man couldn't spread such joy to the world on the third day after Christmas, Cratchit chortled, when 'tis the very season to be jolly, then jovial that man would ever have trouble being.

Cratchit entered his home, and if he could have even been more jolly, it was now. For there bustling about was his own family, arrived back to London surprisingly early. Loud and boisterous as ever, so strong were their feelings for their kin.

"Oh, my dearest wife and all my dear children, how full of heart I am to see you," Bob called out, his happiness such that his own voice was able to reach above the din.

Mrs. Cratchit wrapped her arms round her dear Robert. "We couldn't have stayed a moment more. A vacation is grand, but there's no place like home for the holiday."

"A grand vacation, my foot," Peter coughed, "I'd like to have died of influenza."

"You're lucky, you could have died of boredom, as I did," admonished Belinda. "At least when you spent all day sneezing you had something to do. I would have rather been anywhere in the world."

"Remember, you were with your family, who loves you very much," Tall Tim said to her.

"Is this where you bless me again?" she snipped.

Tim replied far-sharper than expected, making also a blunt remark at the expense of Peter who defended himself, and soon brother, brother and sister were trading ripostes.

Father Cratchit interrupted. "Belinda, my darling daughter, in truth I know where you'd rather have been.

Indeed, where you'd rather be this very moment."

His darling daughter blushed. "How could you?," she asked bewildered, sure her affairs of affection were secret ones from her father.

"It's of no matter. What's of matter is that your heart is with Mr. Pip[25], and where the heart lives the body must be too, such are Life's natural laws. It's of no concern that I believe him a wastrel with poor expectations. Love is blind, the poets say, and the blind are impaired, and the impaired need our love most. Fly to him with my blessing."

"Oh, father!" the girl hugged him. "I shall fly there at once, just as soon as I have kissed you all goodbye, except for Peter for I don't want to catch his illness."

Peter tried to snort his annoyance, "Papa's little girl," but it came across like the late stages of a rasping chest inflammation.

"Peter, my boy," Bob remarked, "your terrible cough could do with a warmer clime, now couldn't it? I plan to send you someplace far more healthy. Like Italy, perhaps. I do believe your lady friend's family vacations there, yes…?"

If Peter could have taken a curative that brought him

---

[25] Pip.

Editor's note: The character of Pip was the model Dickens used for the main character in Great Expectations named Phillip Pirrip, nicknamed "Pip," a youth who blindly pursued his high hopes through life while ignoring the world around him, to his ultimate detriment. By the end of the first paragraph of this Christmas story, Dickens realized that "Phillip Pirrip" was a ridiculous name, and went back to Pip.

instant relief, it would not have worked faster than his father's offer. "You mean that, father?! However did you know?!"

"The truth is it's own answer. Isn't that so, Tall Tim?"

Tim was busy being petulant over his siblings getting rewarded for doing nothing, but allowed that, yes, in truth there is good in us all, which is why we help others this season most of all, the time of goodwill to all men.

Peter and Belinda were too deliriously happy to chide their brother and instead danced about the room. Mrs. Cratchit was delirious, period, at her husband's inexplicable actions and was unsure the family had alighted in the right house.

"No need to do the most good only at this time of year, Tim lad," Bob noted. "And no need for you to one day wear your old braces and crutches as a way to earn charity."

Tim huffed. "I have no intention in the world ever to wear…"

"What would you say to me setting up a charitable foundation through Scrooge & Marley's that you would administer, and at a very nice salary?" Bob interrupted, before his son was caught in a lie he wasn't aware of.

The young man believed he could never believe what he'd just heard. "You have made me speechless," he said with a face so-glowing for all to see. His family cheered, in part for seeing how happy he was, but mostly to know he was actually speechless.

A sound was heard from the front entranceway, and in came the eldest sister, who was astonished to see so many of her siblings dancing around.

"Look who's come home, Bob! It's Martha!" called out

Mrs. Cratchit.

The two young ones raced over. "Hurrah, Martha!" they cried, "Hurrah, hurrah!" And they spun in circles, bumping heads and knocking themselves senseless, except that this presupposes the existence of sense in the first place.

"Martha, dear, it's so nice to have you with the family," expressed Mrs. Cratchit, meaning it, though not fully over the argument with her daughter for leaving the vacation.

"And to think I missed all this," the eldest daughter noted caustically, as she saw two of her siblings dancing around, two others incoherent, another leaping for no known reason, her mother holding a grudge, and her father grinning like a loon.

"Martha, my Martha, what your mother means is that we truly do love having you and your own family a part of ours," Bob explained. "That's why, in the future yet to be, whenever we take a Cratchit vacation, I will pay for separate lodgings at any inn of your choice to assist your struggling family."

"My family isn't struggling in the sli..." Martha stopped. "You will pay for my entire family?? Separate lodgings? Wherever my struggling family wants to stay?"

"Yes, I will."

The young woman threw her arms out. "Mother, dear, it is so good to see you. I missed you so over the holidays. This will make all the difference in the world."

Joy filled the room, except in one corner where Belinda had stopped dancing and now stood sulking. While she was happy for her brothers and sisters, she said, in a tone that left doubt as to its veracity, she noted that Peter had received a trip, Tim a salary, and Martha paid vacations, all she got was permission to leave the house, something she had the right to do as an adult and, come to think of it, was of a mind to exercise permanently.

It was of no account to her father, for he was most happy to accommodate anyone in his family, with the exception of a cousin in Brighton. He emptied his billfold of its bank notes, which were many, gave them to his youngest daughter, and then as good measure handed her the billfold, as well, asking if this would suffice.

Belinda threw her arms around him. "Oh, father, you are the most wonderful there ever was. I could never be upset at you ever again, not ever," an excusable lie given her rush of euphoria and one that had not a single chance of coming to fruition were she to even remember that she had said it.

With four of his children now in throes of ecstasies, the most wonderful father there ever was strode to his two youngest collapsed on the floor breathing heavily following their latest bout of competitive spinning. "And for you two, my youngest dears – here," and he handed them each a piece of hard candy. Oh, my, how their faces lit up with a joy that wouldst make the angels weep.

"Oh, Bob, my dearest, you know I love you deeply," said his good wife, "but honestly, don't you think giving the young ones sugar might be a bit too much for them?

"My dear love, it's three days after Christmas, and as He whose birthday we celebrated three days ago taught us, give and ye shall receive."

All the family agreed that that was profound opinion, though no one was quite sure what any of them would ever receive back from the young ones, other than a pounding headache. But if a pounding headache was good enough for He who was the founder of them all, then it was good enough for them.

"Oh, Bob, my dearest, just seeing our lovely children in such happiness is the finest Christmas present you could ever have given me," the dear lady enthused, thinking too that if it turned out to be the only present she received from him, there would be never-you-mind to pay later on and for a long time to come.

"A family is a family, wherever they are," he warmly sighed. "Far better to have love at a distance, than unhappiness close at hand. Indeed, absence, we are told, makes the heart grow fonder. I look forward to the day when each of our children becomes absent, and we shall then be as happy as a clam." He smiled, and wondered what is was about mollusks that made us attribute great joy to them.

"You could not have said it any better, my dearest Bob," and she hugged him tightly, while tap-tapping her foot on the floor with increased impatience.

What a good woman I married, thought Bob. None is better. I don't care what that McCawber ghost fellow says about his wife. Haunt me for the rest of my life, and I'll not say different, though given a choice, I'd prefer not to be haunted, if it's all the same.

"Light of my life, much as you say you've had the best Christmas gift ever, you deserve more. This very day, I have taken a full-time maid to ease your daily burdens."

Now, that is more like it, thought the best good woman there ever was. "Oh, my dear, Bob," she exclaimed.

139

"You shall never want."

Several moments passed as she waited. Finally realizing that her husband had finished what he was saying, she asked, "Want what?"

"Anything," he explained. "You shall have more than I have given you for many a good year, my good woman. I have great hopes for my firm, and so much aid given to others, yet so many benefits will it bring to those dear to us, including us. Vacations you shall have to see the world, fine clothes for showcasing your beauty, fine china and finer diamonds that will sparkle like your inner love and outer eyes, membership in the best clubs so that the best people may learn that you are best of all. All this and more, for the future yet to be is indeed truly yet to be. "

"That's my Bob!" Mrs. Cratchit cried, with a tear of joy trickling down her cheek. And that is really more like it, she thought. I would have settled for just the maid.

"So, put on the kettle, take out the violin, and we'll celebrate it all over a chalice of Smoking Bishop," he cried.

Mrs. Cratchit smiled at her husband ever-so-dearly. "You can have the Smoking Bishop, my love. I'll drink something else. Anything, actually. And we don't own a violin. But," she added with great kindness and a wink, "we do have a kettle."

"Then that," he shouted with joy, "is where we shall start!"

Bob Cratchit did pretty much everything he said he would. Most he exceeded, but a few were admittedly overly-enthusiastic and not reasonable to hold him to. Bottling Smoking Bishop was one of those, as was a vow to increase profits 2,000% the first year. However, an assemblage of shops that sold fish-and-chips was a significant success throughout the British Isles, and profits did improve by nearly 850% that first year, so he at least approached his promise. Also, he made sure to establish a strong annuity for Scrooge's old fiancé Belle, making up her lost money many times over.

And to his children, who did NOT do anything outlandish to ruin their lives, other than the young ones who in fairness didn't really ruin their lives, but just lived them in their own unique way requiring much parental and occasional medical attention, he was like the father they never had until they had him doing all he wanted. He became as successful an entrepreneur, as successful an investor, and as successful a philanthropist as any success in the London business community knew, or any other business community, marketplace, or commercial center, in the good old financial world.

It is true that some of his fellow magnates laughed at Cratchit for the money he still insisted on giving away through his charitable ventures, but Cratchit didn't mind for he knew that not only did his donations help others immensely and bring much good to society, but they also allowed him to reap additional benefits in taxation credits which aided greatly his many principal industrial enterprises. So, let people laugh, he was laughing himself, all the way to the bank.

Cratchit organized several reunions between himself and the ghosts. Not all the ghosts; Fagin refused to show up. But the rest would get together every while to see one another, usually during the Christmas season, though not on the holiday itself because like as not one of them would have other plans for the day, and on occasion instead they met at random times of the year if that was better for each. Cratchit felt this important, to remain involved with the Spirits because it reminded him of all that he felt one should continually be reminded of, and also if one is involved in serious mercantile pursuits, it didn't hurt to have liaison with those who are aware of the future yet to be and might be able to provide valuable information.

As the paths of his days traveled on, it was always said of Bob that he knew how to run his own business as well as any man alive, and that his egregious success bordered just on the good side of offensive. May that be truly said of us all! And so, as Bob Cratchit observed what Mr. McCawber observed that the good Mrs. McCawber observed, Just Give a Fellow a Stick in his Hand, a Song in his Heart and a Big Sack of Gold! Any season of the entire year! But Christmastime is especially good, oh, my, is it ever!

About the Author

Robert J. Elisberg has been a commentator and contributor to such publications as the Los Angeles *Times*, Los Angeles *Daily News*, *Los Angeles* Magazine, C/NET and E! Online, and served on the editorial board for the Writers Guild of America. He is a regular columnist for the Huffington Post, and has contributed political writing to the anthology, <u>Clued in on Politics</u>, 3rd edition (CQ Press).

Born in Chicago, he attended Northwestern University and received his MFA from UCLA, where he was twice awarded the Lucille Ball Award for comedy screenwriting. Not long afterwards, Elisberg sold his screenplay, *Harry Warren of the Mounties*. He was on staff of the animated series, *Flute Master*, for which he co-write three of the *Skateboy* movies based on the series. He also co-wrote the independent film, *Yard Sale*. Most recently, he wrote the comedy-adventure screenplay, The *Wild Roses*.

Among his other writing, Elisberg co-wrote a book on world travel. Currently, he writes a tech column for the Writers

Guild of America, west. He also co-wrote the song, "Just One of the Girls" for the Showtime movie *Wharf Rat*, and wrote the book for the stage musical, *Rapunzel*.

19481124R00083

Made in the USA
Lexington, KY
19 December 2012